A Year in Beer

The Beer Lover's Guide to the Seasons
Jonny Garrett

CAMRA
BOOKS

**Published by the Campaign
for Real Ale Ltd.**

230 Hatfield Road, St Albans,
Hertfordshire AL1 4LW
United Kingdom
www.camra.org.uk/books

© Campaign for Real Ale Ltd. 2021

ISBN 978-1-85249-372-1

A CIP catalogue record for this book is available from the
British Library
Printed and bound in Slovenia by GPS Group

Commissioning Editor: Katie Button, Alan Murphy
Copy Editor: Alan Murphy
Design/Typography: Hannah Moore
Photography: Jonny Garrett
Cover Design: Callie Jones
Sales & Marketing: Toby Langdon

Many thanks to
This book was written at the height of the COVID-19
pandemic and is dedicated to the NHS and frontline
workers, who kept going when the world stopped. I'd also like
to thank my beautiful wife, Heather – who kept me going
throughout it, too.

Photography by Jonny Garrett. Additional photography by
Brad Evans and Claire Bullen.

Contents

A Year in Beer

Bleary eyed, we **wake** to a **new start**.

Looking for **light in the dark**,

Stepping **around** the **shoots** and **roots**,

Finding **refreshment** in **endless showers**.

Nature comes out of **hibernation**,

Revelling in the new **warmth** of **summer**

And hoping it **lasts forever**.

But the **sun melts away**,

And **everything turns** to gold

As the **sun** starts to **set on the year**.

So we **cling together** for **warmth**,

The world now **lit** by **our own lights**.

Introduction

It's a bold admission for the start of a book about drinking seasonally, but I am not sure that seasonal drinking is really a thing. At least not in the way that most people understand it. Not anymore.

One of the great clichés of beer is that when the autumn arrives, turning the leaves red and your breath to steam, we all start drinking differently. Our magazines and websites are filled with listicles that declare 'The Best Winter Beers' like they are fashionable new coats. En masse, we supposedly drain-pour our Pilsners and Pale Ales to make room for Porters, Stouts and Barley Wines. As with most things, the truth is more complicated.

Until the late 1800s, when scientists discovered the role of yeast in beer and invented refrigeration, brewers were at the mercy of their local climate. Before then, beer fermented at its own pace. In winter it could take months to complete, but in summer it happened so fast that off flavours and infections were common. To make sure there was still enough beer during the thirstiest time of year there would be a rush of brewing in spring, then another at harvest time to replenish the stocks and take advantage of that year's new grain and hops. A lot of beer was made months in advance of being drunk, then laid down to mature in caves or cool cellars and dug up when needed.

The weather also dictated what ingredients were to hand. Malt varied in type and quality, native yeasts worked hot and fast or cold and slow, and all manner of seasonal herbs and spices were used to flavour beer. Combined with the wildly different techniques in brewing, that meant the 'style' of beer would have changed from town to town and month to month. For millennia, seasonal drinking wasn't just one way of experiencing beer: it was the only way.

Things didn't start to change until brewing professionalised. In the Middle Ages most beer making happened in the inns and people's homes, with big landowners and monasteries being the only ones to do it in any volume. When the monasteries were destroyed during the dissolution of the 1600s, dedicated breweries started to spring up throughout the country. These consisted of the 'beer brewers' who used hops, and the 'ale' brewers who barely used any, often preferring the mix of herbs and spices known as gruit. By the 1700s some had grown large enough to ship their beer across the country and even around the empire.

These breweries were the first to spread certain styles and flavours outside of their microclimates, and helped make Britain a brewing powerhouse with a global reputation. Booming domestic and export sales also meant British breweries had money to spend on new technologies, which gave them more control over their beer. They perfected the infusion mash method that meant only one vessel was needed, and started using coke and indirect heat methods to get paler, less smoky malt.

They were all still beholden to the seasons, though, going through annual cycles of intense action and fallow months until the late 1800s. In 1873 Carl Von Linde changed the brewing world when he built the first practical refrigerator system for Munich's Spaten-Franziskaner-Bräu. Until that point, breweries had relied on harvesting ice from lakes and rivers in an attempt to keep cellars cool. That meant a mild winter or a very hot summer could be a disaster. Although expensive, Von Linde's invention meant the brewery could artificially control the temperature of its fermentations and stores in any weather, and even more importantly could finally brew beer all year round.

Just a few years earlier, the French scientist Louis Pasteur had made another vital breakthrough, discovering the roles of yeast and different bacteria in fermentation. While brewers had known the importance of foamy krausen (the bubbly yeast on top of a ferment) for centuries, the actual process – and therefore how best to assist it – had been a source of much debate. A few years later he published his seminal book, *Etudes sur la Bière* (Studies of Beer), in which he spelled out for the first time exactly how beer was spoiled by bacteria. Not only did this lead to his suggestion of holding finished beer at a warm temperature long enough to kill such bacteria (now known as pasteurisation), but it inspired the isolation and spread of certain pure yeast strains amongst thousands of breweries – most notably Carlsberg's Lager yeast, which was named after Pasteur.

Perhaps you can see where this is headed. Before these technological advances from Britain, France and Germany, beer was different wherever you went. Every continent had its history; each region its climate; each brewery its local ingredients and processes; and every brewer their own tastes. That led to wide variations in what it tasted like. But as technology accelerated and travel got easier, these paler beers and cold fermenting yeasts started to spread. Native beer styles and seasonal variation started to blur or even disappear. In 1991 the world's first beer writer, Michael Jackson, put the process very simply: '[It] was only with the development of widespread literacy that the wisdoms – and follies – of uniformity could be learned.'

The age of Pale Lager, and the end of seasonality, was coming.

It was only with the development of **widespread literacy** that the wisdoms – and follies – of uniformity could be learned

The process wasn't quick, but it was pervasive and global. Most famously, Adolphus Busch brought Lager to the US from Bohemia when he created Budweiser. The German-born businessman then created huge networks of ice houses to keep his delivery trucks cold, and embraced pasteurisation to ensure he could deliver across the country. Meanwhile, other German immigrants were bringing Pale Lager to other parts of the world, too – China, Argentina, Brazil and Australia. Wherever it went, it became the dominant style. It could be made with fewer ingredients and survived pasteurisation well, but it was also clear, clean and refreshing, unlike many of the wilder, local styles.

For a long time, Britain resisted. There had always been fashionable or dominant beers here – Brown Ale gave way to Porter, Porter to Mild, and Mild to Bitter. But homogenisation really began to bite after the Second World War. Volumes of the more unusual and stronger dark beers declined so much that they were almost exclusively in bottle by the 1950s. In the modern world change accelerated and Bitter only had around two decades in the spotlight before it came under threat from imported kegged beer. By the start of the seventies some concerned beer geeks had formed the Campaign for Real Ale (CAMRA) to protect the UK's brewing heritage, and while the organisation did a good job of saving cask from obliteration, there was little they could do about the proliferation of Pale Lager.

It started as a flood of Pilsner from Europe. Brands like Stella Artois and Carlsberg grew quickly after their introduction in the 1970s thanks to their cosmopolitan charm and consistent flavour. British breweries jumped on the bandwagon and started producing Lager at home too – whether under licence or through new brands like Courage's Hofmeister. Pale Lager was just 2% of the market in 1965, but hit 50% in 1985 and topped out at 75% at the end of 2008. Combined with a bloodbath of takeovers and closures that saw hundreds of heritage British brands wiped from the face of the earth, British brewing was unrecognisable by the 1990s. The Burtons, Milds, Porters and Stouts that define our history were regional curiosities, as were traditions such as wet hop beers and old ales. The cooperage craft was dying and our hop farms were being converted to more profitable crops. The notion of seasonality – even diversity – in British beer was all but lost.

Since you're reading this book, you probably know what happened next. A new tax break for small brewers, consumer frustration at the lack of choice, and shockwaves from the American craft beer revolution revived the industry. We went from just a few hundred breweries in 2002 to around 2,500 two decades later, breathing life into the crumbling industrial areas and railway arches of our cities. But sheer numbers don't always mean diversity.

We went from just a **few hundred** breweries in 2002 **to around 2,500** two decades later

The craft beer boom has brought back countless styles and conceived new ones, but it hasn't yet brought back seasonality. Technology and globalisation have spoiled us, and beer geeks' appetite for pale, American-hopped beer isn't diminished by changes in the weather. Brewers import their hops from climates entirely different to our own, store malts all year round, and order their yeast from a laboratory. They can ferment beers at any temperature they want, then store and transport them cold to drinkers who are protected from the elements like never before. When it's cold we put the heating on, and when we want a chilled Pilsner we just go to the fridge.

Despite the whole world's beer culture now being at our fingertips, we are drawn to just a few styles and hardly influenced by the seasons at all. The idea that suddenly every pint poured in the pub is dark, roasty and warming come winter just doesn't play out in the reality. Most of us just drink our favourite Bitters, IPAs and German Pilsners come rain or shine.

It's likely that some people are shaking their head violently while reading this and, depending on the season, drinking exactly what the temperature dictates. This

SITE OF
ANCHOR BREWERY
LIST OF BREWERS
THE MONGER FAMILY 1616–1670
JOSIAH CHILD 1670–1693
EDMUND HALSEY M.P. 1693–1729
RALPH THRALE 1729–1758
HENRY THRALE 1758–1781
BARCLAY, PERKINS & CO.
1781–1955
COURAGE LTD.
1955–1986

PARK STREET

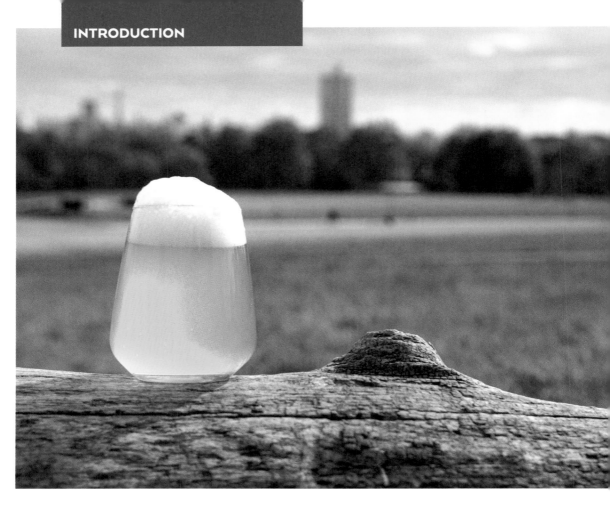

book is dedicated to these wonderful people, but also aimed at those who have not discovered the joy of seasonal drinking. Because making a connection between the world around us and the beer we drink is a powerful revelation. Seasonal drinking might not be a thing, but wouldn't it be brilliant if it was?

You see, while modern technology has reduced the seasons' impact on what we brew, it has done something else too. It's made brewers so good at making clean, shelf-stable beer that every style under the sun can now be found in pubs and bottleshops all year round. That allows us drinkers the opportunity to create that connection with the seasons ourselves.

So what does seasonal drinking mean in a world where we can brew, drink and eat whatever we want, whenever we want? The answer lies in our past, and the imprint it has left on us and our culture. It's about geography, sociology and technology. On the one hand it's global, bringing in the economy, trade routes and politics. And on the other hand it's deeply personal – it depends on our personalities, our mood, what music is playing, and what we're having for dinner.

Today we can taste what winter was like in North Germany 200 years ago, or what summer is like in Florida in 2020. We can transport ourselves, or ground ourselves right where we are. All we need to do is understand how, and more importantly why, we do it.

When we analyse beer we usually reference three senses: we look at light through the beer, inhale the aroma, and savour the flavours. But really we're using all of our myriad senses. We can feel its temperature relative to the room; hear the fizz of the bottle and the chatter around us; we read others' emotions and reactions; we perceive time slowing down or speeding up. All these things set synapses in our brains firing with emotions and memories – and that nostalgia makes connections between seemingly disparate things. A smoked beer made near Manchester reminds me of the Bonfire Nights of my childhood in Oxford; a Helles from Hartlepool reminds me of a glorious summer spent in the parks of East London; a Flemish Red from Somerset leaves me hankering for a rich beef stew and open fire I remember from Cornwall. It's this vital context that, on top of the colour, aroma and flavour, makes us decide what beer is best and when.

That's really what this book is about – neither beer in isolation, nor even beer in relation to the seasons. Really it's about beer at the point that everything around it converges. As we go through the year we'll note how the natural and human world around us changes completely, and how our brewing and drinking habits can change subtly to suit them. We'll look at how winter encourages the production of beer styles intertwined with nature; how the abundance of spring inspires unique aromas in our brewing; how summer turns drinking into a team sport; and how autumn connects to our home and our memories. All through that we'll see how humans adapted to the limitations and opportunities of living in a pre-industrial age, and how the annual rhythms of the past still affect us.

Hopefully, you're starting to see what I'm getting at. Our notions of drinking seasonally, even the seasons themselves, go well beyond mercury levels and precipitation graphs. We don't drink Imperial Stout in November because it's cold – we have central heating and double glazing! No, we drink Imperial Stout in November because the brewers brew it out of tradition, because our ancestors had to drink it then, because it's a dark beer and it's dark outside, because it suits the food we're tucking into, because we need to drink the one we bought back in August, and maybe because we read books that told us to. Our reactions can be unexpected, too. We might chase the taste of summer and have a Pilsner, or miss autumn so have a pumpkin beer. It's why we all put our winter coats on a few weeks too early, and barbecue in the rain during spring.

This is what modern seasonal drinking is: an emotive way of connecting our beer and ourselves with the world around us. In this book we'll look at the history of brewing and drinking, and how our culture has been shaped by it to make this new idea of seasonality.

It's time to explore a year in beer.

January

There's no hangover like the one we endure as a nation on 1 January. Mingled with the leftover taste of beer is the guilt that this is supposed to be a new chapter in our lives. This was the year we were going to change, and yet here we are laid out on the sofa eating crisps and hoping our head clears in time for work the next day. We are in the darkest dead of winter, and the hope of spring is still hidden under the earth. And so we have to go digging.

If you look hard enough there is a lot to love about January. For me, it's about embracing the slower pace of life for a few weeks, putting faith in the promise of what's to come. It feels fitting that January is a vital month in the brewing of spontaneous, Lambic-style beer. Once brewed, these wild ales must be chilled naturally overnight, and January has plenty of nights that are cold enough. The liquid is then piped into barrels where it will lie undisturbed, fermenting and funk-ifying for up to three, four or even five New Year celebrations before being blended. It is the perfect metaphor for the month – with little happening now, we can lay the foundations to the future.

Perhaps that's why we like to cut back in January, with many people choosing to stop drinking altogether. This human-induced seasonal abstinence has never made much sense to me, but doing it one year did lead me to the discovery of table beer and in particular a six-month-matured 2% Lager from Small Beer Co.

On that note, there's also usually a glut of full-strength Lagers released in January, as brewers fill their tanks with something that can mature for a few weeks while they take a well-earned Christmas break. The thought of these beers all over the country, hibernating in steel jackets throughout the festive period, always brings a smile to my face. It may be slow, but it's a new start all the same.

What to drink

This is traditionally the time to cut back after the excesses of Christmas, and if you've got the strength you'll be delighted to know there are now hundreds of fantastic low-alcohol beers on the market. Hopheads look out for Northern Monk Holy Faith, Lager lovers should reach for Lucky Saint, and anyone looking for a mix of styles should get a mixed case from Nirvana Brewing or Big Drop Beer Co. Personally, I prefer to cut back just a few percentage points and enjoy some great table beers – Small Beer Co, The Kernel and The Beak Brewery make the best for my money.

There's also that rush of cold-matured beers at the start of the year too, so look to the UK's great Lager breweries for something special. If that's not enough to excite the beer geek in you, January is also the time that Verdant Brewing Co release their much-vaunted Double IPA, Putty. The heavy use of Galaxy hops means it benefits from plenty of time mellowing over Christmas, and it is released just in time to be the perfect way to fall off the wagon at midnight on the 31st.

What to eat

Given that it's the season of wholesome health, it's convenient that many delicious vegetables come into, or remain, in season in January. Roasted or mashed celeriac is a great winter side, and nothing says 'well, at least there's veg in it' like a big spoonful of cheesy leeks. Leek and potato soup is, perhaps, a more sensible choice, but I'd prefer a roast parsnip one with some Indian spices to get you sweating through the colds.

Where to go

Britain's pubs really struggle in January – especially those focused on beer rather than food – but with everyone saving money while shedding the pounds, takings go down across the board. So, even if you're doing Dry January, get down to your local as much as you can anyway. There should be lots of soft and low-alcohol options to enjoy, and I promise you will never be more appreciated by your landlord than you are in the coldest month of the year.

This is traditionally the time to cut back after the excesses of Christmas, and if you've got the strength you'll be delighted to know there are now hundreds of fantastic **low-alcohol** beers on the market

The Champagne of Brussels

Ring in the New Year with Gueuze

These days we're most likely to pop the Champagne at New Year, but there was a time when every celebration in the UK was marked with beer. Whether it was a birthday, an engagement, a religious holiday or the end of a war, we cracked open the casks and drank by the pint.

For the first few hundred years it was simply because beer was the only choice in Britain, certainly for the lower classes. A lot of the beer drunk up until the Middle Ages would have been made at home, but monasteries also brewed and sold it to fund their way of life. The dissolution put paid to that tradition, and brewing started to professionalise. Then, in 1830, the government introduced the Beer House Act, which meant that for a fee of around two guineas (£250 in today's money) anyone could brew and sell beer. Within a decade more than 45,000 beer houses, many of which were breweries, had opened up – one for every 400 people. If beer wasn't our national drink before, then it certainly took that title then.

Despite what it looks like, the aim was actually to reduce drunkenness. There was a fear among the ruling classes that strong spirits such as gin were bringing ruin to the workers. By making beer so readily available (and therefore cheaper) it was hoped that Britain's loyalties would shift back to beer. It's certainly an interesting theory, but judging by the history books, people still gave getting drunk a bloody good go. They found any excuse for a great feast and piss-up and local beer was at the centre of it all. It seems that these feasts were moments where the feudal system broke down a little, at least for the day. Generally, a wealthy landowner would brew the beer and host the event for his tenants and workers, and a day of celebration would ensue. Most famous were the workhouse Christmas parties, where the master would put on a feast of admirable proportions, including roast beef, plum pudding and at least one pint of ale for the women and two for the men.

My favourite excuse for a beer festival, however, was the Coming of Age party. In the mid-19th century, when a new heir was born to a landowner he would have his household brew a special strong beer that was then laid down until the boy turned twenty-one. On that day the beer would finally be cracked and served at a great feast, with all the locals and workers invited. These events got pretty wild because the beers were absurdly strong. The original gravities regularly reached 1.110. If that means nothing to you, by the time the wild yeasts had gone to town on that amount of sugar for twenty-one years, you'd have a beer of at least 13% ABV.

British history is littered with outrageous receipts for the sale of beer at important events, but after the Second World War that started to change. Wine took beer's place at the table, and Champagne stole its role in celebration, leaving beer with the mini victories, such as 'thank god it's Friday', or 'it's time we caught up'. One of the things I love about a pint of beer is that it doesn't need an occasion, but beer is also brilliant at making moments even more special. No other beverage on earth has the intrinsic variation that beer does through its magical formula of malt, hops, yeast and water. Sure, it can be a simple Pale Lager, drunk ice cold and straight from the bottle, but if you want a beer with a cork and cage that goes pop when you open it, a beer that's dry as a bone with complex notes of oak, flowers and citric fruit, then there's still a beer for you. In fact, there are lots of beers like that, and they make better celebratory drinks than fizzy wine. The most famous is Gueuze, which is even known as the 'Champagne of Brussels'.

That might be a little self-aggrandizing, but the process is equally laborious and the origins echo each other. Champagne was never meant to be fizzy – the first wines made in the region were an attempt to rival those of Burgundy. Unfortunately, the lower temperatures further north (and perhaps some inexperience) meant that fermentation didn't always complete before the wine was bottled. As a result, some

of those wines fermented a little further in bottle, creating carbonation under pressure. This was initially seen as a flaw by winemakers and drinkers, especially on the occasions when the bottles exploded and injured people. It took an Englishman to work out exactly what was happening, with Christopher Merret publishing a paper in 1662 on the residual presence of sugar being responsible for refermentation and carbonation. By then, however, some French and indeed English aristocracy had decided they quite liked the bubbles, and glass production had improved enough that exploding bottles were very unlikely.

It's a similar story for Gueuze, which is a blend of Lambic, a style of beer that is one of the last remaining relics of how all beer used to be made. Until the late 1800s brewers weren't aware of the role that yeast played in making alcohol, but they knew that if they transferred the gloopy sediment from one fermentation to the next it would result in pretty consistent beer. Not every brewery did this though – some got the results they were after just by leaving the malty brew to cool overnight, before transferring to barrels. There, the wild yeasts in the air, within the brewery and in the barrels themselves, would ferment the beer over several years. That's how the Lambics of the Senne Valley near Brussels were made, and how they're still made today.

The origin of Gueuze is a little murky. The popular theory is that the carbonation was an accident embraced by an unnamed Lambic brewer on Rue Des Geux in Brussels in the mid-1800s. There are a few issues with this theory though. For one, there's no such Rue in Brussels (though there is a Place Des Geux), and for two, many of the first references to Gueuze are in barrel. It also seems that neither version was blended, and Gueuze was originally just a well-aged and expensive

Gueuze – which has to be a bottled blend of one-, two- and three-year Lambic – **can deliver a lot more complexity** than any Champagne I have tried

Lambic showing more funky cider-like complexity and less sweetness.

There's little doubt that some of these beers would have carbonated in bottle as the wild yeasts ate the remaining sugar, but most would have remained flat. It's pretty likely that, having seen the excitement around sparkling Champagne, Belgian brewers started experimenting with blending to achieve the same effect – adding young Lambic with more sugar left over to ensure secondary fermentation. Whatever the inspiration, it was soon crowned the Champagne of Brussels, and it can't have been coincidence that it came in the same corked bottles.

It may have been a tribute act, but Gueuze – which now has to be a bottled blend of one-, two- and three-year Lambic according to EU law – can deliver a lot more complexity than any Champagne I have tried. Its wild yeasts and microbes, gathered from the air of Brussels and oak barrels that have seen hundreds of past batches, add all kinds of flavours. There's stone fruit and pear from the standard brewing cultures, hay, pineapple and scrumpy from the Brettanomyces yeasts, and soft, lemon acidity and sherbet from the Lactobacillus and Pediococcus. Let's add that to the digestive biscuit, honey and oat cracker notes of the malt bill, the soft bitterness of the aged hops, and the little scratch of oak from the barrel, then finally muse over the magic that comes from combining it into one super-effervescent drink. Great Gueuze feels modern but connects us to brewing processes and traditions that stretch back millenia.

Its complexity is why it's such a special drink, but it's also why Gueuze nearly died out during the 20th century while Champagne became the popping cork of choice around the world. The rise of 'clean' fermented beer – in particular Pilsner, with its glorious simplicity – made things extremely tough for a style that's still an acquired taste. By the 1990s there were only a handful of Lambic breweries left, and to suit modern palates most had sweetened their beers so much that they were unrecognisable. Lindemans, which was founded in 1822, had seen mainstream success from its range of sweetened and heavily fruited Lambics, but they also kept the traditional Lambic styles alive. Today you can still try its incredible Oude Cuvée René, which is a beautiful example of what a true Gueuze should be, and the Oude Kriek Cuvée René is dark, deep and cherry-filled.

Thankfully, the growth of craft beer has helped save Lambic from ignominy. The birth of beer geek forums on the internet meant these niche beers suddenly had interest from all over the world, and breweries like Cantillon and Drie Fonteinen are worshipped and sought after in every corner of the globe.

That resurgence led to several exciting new breweries springing up and nowadays there's enough variation in Lambic to keep us drinking it throughout the year, not just during the brewing season: there's the flatter, highly fruited and acidic blends of Hanssens; the fresh and dialled-in 'moon' apricot Lambics of Bofkont; and the four-year time capsule that is Drei Fonteinen's Golden Blend. Rappers aren't hosting lavish parties with unlimited Tilquin Gueuze, and bankers aren't buying corners of barley fields to ensure supply, but there are beer traders in America who will pay hundreds of dollars on the grey market for the rarer Cantillons.

While these breweries are fiercely against the secondary market that has sprung up around them, most are now lucky enough to sell everything they make with ease. As they slowly expand to meet demand they are also experimenting more, which means plenty more options for beer lovers refusing to settle for the predictable bubbles at new year. For me, Boon Black Label offers absurd value and incredible complexity that makes it a great party beer – its vintages have a really modern citrus hit to them, which might make it more approachable to those unsure about the edginess that Gueuze has. The unsweetened cherry and kriek lambics also make fantastic gateways to the world of lambic – fresh Cantillon's Rose De Gambrinus is like liquid raspberry jam and Oude Beersel's Oude Kriek is like a cherry Bakewell. The variety of flavours means there is so much you can do with food matching, too – try a Framboise with smoked salmon blinis, Krieks are fantastic with goat's cheese tarts, and Gueuze is delicious with mushroom vol-au-vents (yeah it's still the eighties in my house). If you're looking for something that still has that fresh grape skin note, you can even now find wonderful grape-aged lambics like Tilquin's Pinot Noir and Pinot Gris and Cantillon's Vigneronne. These beers and matches are so good that even a sceptic might admit there's something to admire underneath those wilder flavours.

So from my tiny corner of the world, where beer is everything, it feels long past time that the Champagne of Brussels was given its place as a celebratory drink. No year in beer should start without it.

There are **beer traders** in America who will pay **hundreds of dollars** on the grey market for the rarer Cantillons

Spontaneous beer

Isn't really all that spontaneous

Stood on a mezzanine above the brewing floor of Burning Sky is what looks like a four-poster bed. The legs are old pine, but the roof is made from the staves of barrels that once contained Girardin Lambic. The base, where the mattress would sit, is filling with boiling hot wort, releasing waves of sticky caramel, freshly mown grass and the unmistakable tang of hops.

Burning Sky's coolship used to be in the barn next door, but it's much more impressive here in the main building, where it lords over the rows of steel fermenters that contain the brewery's clean beers. The steam that rises from the fresh wort cascades over the edge like a waterfall, filling the room with thick aroma.

It's the fourth year that Burning Sky has brewed with its coolship, which means they have also just released their first Gueuze-style beer made with three different ages of spontaneous beer. To mark the occasion of this brew, a bottle of Coolship No 3 is passed around. It has foamy sherbet, lemon, wild flowers and pepper, as well as plenty of farmyard and cider-like funk and a sharp, stinging-nettle finish. It conjures up images of the sleepy, slate-lined village of Firle where Burning Sky is situated. I think the beer is truly stunning, but as we sip our small pours, Burning Sky founder Mark Tranter is poker faced. It's 'developing' is all he'll really say.

Until recently, Lambic-style brewing has been the preserve of a particular part of Belgium to the south-west of Brussels. But today breweries all around the world brew mixed-fermentation beers inspired by this unique beer culture. I say inspired by, because the local ingredients and processes used mean that these beers taste different depending on where and when they were made. The EU protects the processes so you can't call it Lambic unless you do it as the Belgians do, but that doesn't mean beautiful Lambic-like beer can't be made in other ways. Burning Sky uses a little genuine Lambic from Girardin in their blends, but the brewery mostly produces its own wild wort and, unshackled by the traditions of true Lambic brewing, have departed a fair way from the recipe and the processes observed by the Belgians. Four years of brewing one beer may sound like all the practice you need, but the team is still experimenting. This year the wort includes rye and spelt on top of the classic wheat and pale malt, and this time Mark also throws in some stuffed cotton bags. What he stuffs them with I cannot say: I am sworn to secrecy.

Some traditions remain, though. Coolships were once the quickest way to cool a beer, and most breweries used them regardless of what styles they were brewing. The wide and shallow basins gave as much surface area as possible for the heat to escape. Of course, a larger surface area also meant more chance that local and wild yeast and bacteria would infect the beer. That was more likely in summer, which is why brewing stopped pretty much all over Europe in the warmer months, and spontaneous brewing still only ever happens in winter (or spring at a push).

Most brewers tried to limit any infection by pitching healthy yeast from a previous brew to eat the sugars before the wild bacteria could take hold. But not the Lambic brewers – they relied entirely on this natural inoculation, and even encouraged it. They used a special method to create long-chain sugars that are harder for standard brewing yeasts to ferment. The technique, known as a 'turbid mash', leaves plenty of food for the wilder yeast and bacteria to work on, but it also means more work for the brewers.

The turbid mash should really be called a torture mash. It involves several temperature steps, achieved by repeatedly separating and boiling portions of the mash before re-adding them over several hours. This is then followed by a four- or even five-hour boil, and the caramelisation from both processes means only the hungriest of yeasts can break down the sugars. Although Mark has condensed it down to a two-hour mash and 90-minute boil, they still go through most of this arduous process to keep at least a little influence on the fermentation. For the first few batches, the Burning Sky team watched on nervously as some barrels refused to start fermenting for weeks. In brewing a clean beer that would be a disaster, but for wild barrel-aged beer it could even be an advantage.

Each barrel has its own character, created by what was in it before and even where it is in the brewery – influences like the amount of sunlight, temperature and humidity will cause variations between fermentation in barrels that brewers can either round out or accentuate through blends. A barrel near the door that catches the light might develop more acetic vinegar character, while funky brett might really take hold in a barrel in a dark corner. Both would be unbalanced and two dimensional on their own, but could add nuance and depth to each other if blended. Perhaps the red wine tannins were really pronounced in an old Bordeaux barrel, but almost non-existent in a Pinot Noir one – a little of both will create the right level of complexity.

If consistency is hard to create with these beers, predictability is still important, and as Burning Sky has refined the process, fermentation has sped up and become more reliable. I visited just a week after the first coolship brew of the season, and it was already fermenting vigorously. The small sample I was offered was heavily perfumed with isoamyl acetate – basically foam bananas – which is the sign of either a Hefeweizen yeast or, more likely here, a hot and fast ferment.

That remarkable early aroma won't last long. With easy sugars to work on and the temperatures still cold, the cleaner microbes will rule to start with, but as the heat ramps up in early summer the wilder elements will take hold.

Thanks to the turbid mash and long boil, the bacteria and Brett character will go to town all the way through to winter. At that point it will have a little acidity and funk but still plenty of sweetness. In Belgium people drink it at this age (they call it Jonge Lambic), but it's more likely to be matured through several seasonal cycles, or used as the young portion of a Gueuze and aged as part of that blend.

Burning Sky's bottles are too young for us to know how they will age, but it's not the only UK brewery making these kinds of beers. Every winter a handful of breweries around the country fill their coolships with some form of turbid mashed wort. Each one is radically different from the other thanks to the different processes and locations of the brewery. Wild Beer Co in Somerset makes wonderfully fresh-tasting spontaneous beer, with a crisp apple-like note that perhaps comes from being surrounded by orchards. A lot of the yeast used to make fine cider will end up in their beers, bringing that same character to all three of the blends they've released so far. Mills Brewing is in another famous cider region, Herefordshire, but its first blend, Today, has more lemon acidity and wheaty character. The brewery sticks strictly to the traditional Belgian process, with a five-step mash and four-hour boil, and as such has ended up with a blend that comes the closest of all the UK brewers to true Lambic. Up in Scotland, Fyne Ales' first three-year blend, Home, is the least acidic. Instead it has lots of orange peel and sherry flavours that make it feel older than the other blends. Perhaps the cooler Argyll temperatures have muted the wild character to create a smoother palate.

All these beers have the potential to age beautifully, but only time will tell us exactly how they change. The shifts will be slow and subtle: after all, the beer has already changed so much during its years in barrel. To me, the joy of a well-aged wild ale isn't how much it changes, but stays the same. Its unique local flavour can remind us of places we've been and times we've shared, bringing it all back years later like a faded photograph. I've spent years talking about spontaneous beers, but I never really understood the incredible connection they have with their locale and this time of year until I stood up on that mezzanine and watched the beer meet the cold air for the first time. I look forward to tasting it in three years' time, in an entirely different part of the world, and being transported straight back to that moment and that place.

All these beers have **the potential to age beautifully,** but only time will tell us exactly how they change. The shifts will be slow and subtle

Dry January

And how to make that feeling last all year

'January is bleak enough without giving up beer.'

That's a line I used to thoroughly enjoy trotting out once a year, whenever I was asked about the Dry January campaign, which was born out of the charity now known as Alcohol Change UK.

On the surface it looks like an excellent time to abstain. Christmas is decadent and expensive, so it's the only time of the year where you might actually want a break from indulgence. Not only that, but the whole 'New Year, New You' marketing thing is in full swing across our culture. At this point, it's almost expected of us.

But in reality the days are short, the weather oppressive and the Christmas comedown sudden. Winter without Christmas to look forward to can be so slow that it sometimes feels like the world has stopped turning, and there's so little to do with your time that removing a well-tested way of passing it – drinking – seems madness. But that was before I was offered money to do it.

In a mad moment while writing this book, most likely during a hangover, I had pitched to a magazine editor the idea of a Dry January diary, chronicling my experiences of giving up alcohol for the first time in a decade. Unfortunately he jumped at the idea, so I started preparing for thirty-one days completely sober.

The fact that I'd lose my hobby and a large portion of my job aside, I was also worried about how my body would react. I drink around five times a week, usually doubling the UK government's recommended weekly guidelines of 14 units. I understand those units are based on the 'average person', and my thirty-something keen-cyclist body is clearly different to a, say, sixty-year-old obese woman in terms of risk, but the temperance lobby has done such a number on me that I even contacted an addiction specialist to check this was a sensible thing to do. She told me at the levels I was drinking the only real risk I ran was high blood pressure, and that short-term I was unlikely to feel anything other than better rested.

She was right. While I had some pretty wild dreams (you spend more time in REM when alcohol isn't disrupting your sleep cycle) and a staring competition with a bottle of Barley Wine halfway through, I had plenty to distract me while on the wagon. The range of low-alcohol beers available now is staggering, and during my month off I managed to drink examples of Pilsner, Helles, English Pale Ale, American Pale Ale, IPA, New England IPA, Hefeweizen, Berliner Weisse, Porter, Stout and even Pastry Stout. The quality varied, but that's true of full-strength brewing too, and by the end I had found two beers that I still stock in my fridge for nights off. In Germany one in every fifteen beers sold is low alcohol, so it's no wonder most of them are excellent, but Rothaus's Tannenzapfle Alkoholfrei is so close to the real thing I checked the label the first time I tried it. If you're after something hoppy, Northern Monk Brewing's Holy Faith is a little thinner and drier than the original Faith, but it still carries that juicy aroma and aftertaste.

By the end of the month I was fully prepared to declare low-alcohol beer a revelation. But in reality, the only revelation was the Beak Brewery Bohemian Pilsner I had carefully chosen to be my first beer. The incredible depth of flavour and finish was unlike anything I had consumed in the previous thirty days. Dry January had shown me that low-alcohol beer had its place, but as close as the very best ones get, they can never be the same as a fully fermented one. There will always be something missing.

That's true however they're made, but the different methods do have subtly different results, particularly between those that remove the alcohol and those that prevent it being created in the first place. The most common method is arrested fermentation, where the brewer mashes the grain so hot that only a tiny fraction of the malt's sugars become fermentable. It's the cheapest option and can leave 'worty'

sweetness, but has the benefit of nothing being stripped from the beer later on. The other two main approaches involve removing the alcohol: one via reverse osmosis and the other by distillation. Whatever the method, however, you're not simply stripping a beer of its alcohol, and nor are you just making it a little thinner and drier – you're removing something less tangible too, a complexity you can taste but can't express. In the video diary I made I called it spiritual but after hours of research it turned out to be highly scientific.

In brewing there are a few key chemical processes. Beer's flavour comes from extracting body and colour from the malt, then bitterness and aroma from the hops. Most of that happens during the mash and the boil, which are done at high temperatures to aid the process. But ask any brewer and they will tell you that a lot of the beer's character only begins to develop during fermentation – in other words, once alcohol is present along with the hop and malt flavour compounds.

Ethanol is the main form of alcohol in beer, and it's an excellent flavour extractor. I could go into the science of why, but it's easier just to demonstrate with a seasonal example. Add some sloe berries to water and leave it for a few weeks and you'll come back to some ever so slightly fragrant water. Do the same with gin, and you'll have a rich red liquid, steeped in deep sloe flavours. This process of extraction is the same with hops and malt in beer – without alcohol you won't achieve that same saturation of flavour, and whether you boil or filter to make a low-ABV beer, it's not just the alcohol you lose. So, despite the wide variety of exciting and tasty low-alcohol beers, for me the most exciting development in the British beer world for this time of year has been the rise of table beers.

Most beer around the world sits between 4% and 5%. In the UK it's at the bottom end of that spectrum, and we've developed a pint culture that suits it. In fact, we've evolved to a four-or-five-pint culture based on the wonderfully flawed logic that because it's half the alcohol of something like wine, we can have twice as much. It's for that reason – and the sudden popularity of 8% Double IPAs – that table beers have become popular.

Where a table wine is a less complex bottle that can be enjoyed with food, a table beer is a low-ABV brew that was historically enjoyed at mealtimes by the entire family. It would have been around 2% or 3%, making it hard to get drunk on, but safer and more delicious than most water sources. Most commercial examples were made using the third runnings of the mash, washing off the very last of the malt sugars to make a thin and very light ale that was likely hopped with spent flowers from a previous, more expensive beer. As a result, it wasn't so much a style because its colour, flavour and strength depended entirely on what the main brew had been.

Today it's very different. Modern techniques and ingredients allow brewers to make full-flavoured and full-bodied beers at remarkably low ABVs, using the first runnings of extra hot mashes to get lots of body but less sugar, and big, late-addition hops to bring alluring aromas without bitterness. As a result, these new table beers can taste a lot like their bigger siblings.

What's great about that is how, perhaps more than any other beer a brewery makes, it cuts to the core of their personality – it's their approach in miniature, and being so light it leaves everything exposed. Verdant's People, Money, Space, Time is

a snip at just 3.8% but it carries so much of the brewery's love of thick body and over-saturated hop character. In contrast, Gadd's incredible 1.2% IPA is cracker dry and full of fresh grass and bramble fruits that remind me of late British summertime. Kernel's Table beer has the look of a New England IPA but there's plenty of grain character, fresh citrus and a cleansing bitter finish. Five Points Brewery's Micro Pale is dry as London Fields in August, but layered with floral notes. Burning Sky's Petite Saison is a 3.5% zippy, lemony pale that spends a few months in wine barrels to turn tart and gain remarkable depth. Each of these beers speaks uniquely of the brewery that made it, and the different styles they'd want to drink day-in day-out like our ancestors.

Table beer wasn't the only low-alcohol beer available historically, though. Small beer was a term used for weak and cheap beer at the time and, until 1802, was taxed even less than table beer. This was drunk all day, not just at meal times, to fortify a poor workforce almost entirely employed in manual labour.

While we don't have quite the lifestyle of an 18th-century factory worker or farmer, one UK brewery still sees value in the concept of the small beer – one that can be enjoyed at lunch, at work, or for a night out. Small Beer Co's strongest beer is their Steam Beer, at a tiny 2.7%. Completing the line-up is a 2.5% Pale Ale, 2.1% Lager and 1% Dark Lager. All the beers are light and crisp, but thanks to using entire mashes and undergoing full fermentation – including six weeks of cold conditioning for the two Lagers – they are full-flavoured and refreshing.

Co-founder and head brewer Felix James is an ex-Fuller's brewer, and says coming up with the recipes was easy – it's the special processes to ensure body and flavour at such low strengths that's difficult. At a glance the brewhouse looks a lot like every other in the country, but on closer inspection there are extra brewing vessels and strange panels in the mash tun floor. It's here that Felix says the magic happens – where a weak beer can be given strong flavour, colour and depth. He's coy on the details, but says it's down to how he layers the malts in the tun. Most breweries simply mill the grain ad hoc and combine it all, stirring to ensure it's all mixed together. But Felix places certain grains in exact positions to change what the liquid filters through, and at what time and temperature.

It's a lot of effort for such a niche part of the market, but after three years – one of which was a pandemic – the company is starting to get its message out there. Small Beer isn't the more polite side of any temperance movement, in fact it's not really about reducing how much we drink at all. For me, and I think for Felix, it's all about the moment of drinking and maintaining the right balance between lucid thinking and that lovely two-pint buzz for as long as possible. He regales me with the first time his beers were put on draught in a few London Fuller's pubs. To celebrate, he and his team went for a pub crawl of their new customers, and despite visiting around ten and having a pint in each, he claims he woke up without a hangover or any regrets.

What I love about Felix's beers – as well as many of the table beers I've tried – is that they give me the hedonism of alcohol and the escapism of a few pints, while still cutting back. Now I just have to stop telling myself I can have twice as many.

Looking for
light
in the
dark

February

January may be the month we all fail at our resolutions, but it's also a month of hope and new beginnings. February that follows, however, has none of that optimism. Instead you're left scrabbling around in the dark to find your own.

When I need to do that I have four places I look first: family, friends, food and beer. The first two are self-explanatory, and the second two are how you lure them in. We don't just celebrate, we commiserate with good food and drink, and it being February is as good an excuse as any. We can do that at home, perhaps while we celebrate Pancake Day, St Valentine's Day and – most important in my eyes – National Pizza Day, or we can get out there for long frosty walks that finish with supporting our local pubs and restaurants.

The puritanism of January is dispensed with, and there's no gnawing guilt at indulging ourselves. In this bleak month when nothing is happening and it's too cold to really be outside for long, the pub is the perfect meeting place – especially one with an open fire, lots of classic Bitter on the cask pumps, and maybe a piano in the corner.

The trees may be bare and lifeless, but there is so much living to do inside.

What to drink

If you've just finished Dry January, then you shouldn't deny yourself some of the most hype-inducing, silly and exciting beer you can find. If you've not put yourself through that, then for me February is the time for lots of sessionable beer. Cask is also the order of the day, being served a few degrees warmer than most keg beer. Classic British Bitters and Porters offer the right kind of flavours for the season and are hearty after a cold walk, while hoppy table beers and Session IPAs can give you a blast of summer when you need it. It's also still spontaneous beer brewing season, so it would be rude not to crack some Lambic or Lambic-style beer.

What to eat

February isn't exactly abundant, but there are some early spring vegetables shooting out of the ground. Jerusalem artichokes are a nightmare to prepare but delicious when deep fried Roman-style and served with a lemony Lager or Gueuze. Forced rhubarb is also in season, so get it in your pies or crumbles, and serve it with a fruited Sour. If you prefer things a little sweeter you could even choose a Sour with lactose in it. There is, of course, the delicious and messy affair of Pancake Day to deal with too – and beer can play a pivotal role in that as we'll find out.

Where to go

There are usually two big beer festivals in February. The first is CAMRA's Great British Winter Beer Festival, which is given a cosy feel by the range of seasonal beers. It's by no means a dark beer festival though, with nearly as much variation as the main August event.

The other is Cloudwater Brew Co's Friends & Family & Beer, which is just about the geekiest festival in the UK. You'll be treated to a well-balanced but startlingly star-studded brewery line-up, and also some of Manchester's best street food. Cask Festival is usually the same weekend, a celebration of modern real ale run by the founders of London's Affinity Brew Co. Expect lots of experimentation as well as traditional brewing, all served in the CAMRA-approved fashion.

Classic British **Bitters and Porters** offer the right kind of flavour for the season and are hearty after a cold walk, while hoppy **table beers and Session IPAs** can give you a blast of summer

The best of Bitters

A beautiful style with a bad name

One of the most common clichés about British beer is that it's warm and flat. Anyone who believes that has been drinking in the wrong pubs.

The cask ales that this cliché refers to are indeed less carbonated than most kegs, but a flat one is flawed and should be taken back to the bar. Cask beers are also served a little warmer, but still they should all be noticeably chilled – around 10°C. That's roughly the temperature of the English Channel at this time of year and if you consider that warm, feel free to take a long swim in it.

Still, its warmer temperature does make cask a wonderful fit for the coldest month of the year, and a Bitter is my cask style of choice. A good one is bittersweet and hearty, with nourishing bread and honey notes, but also a low ABV that encourages long sessions in warm pubs. At this time of year I'm surprised to see people drinking anything else. That said, a classic regional British Bitter has become harder and harder to find over the last decade. While the recipes have remained the same, the word breweries use to describe them has shifted. Today, few of the biggest beers are actually branded Bitter at all.

Shepherd Neame Spitfire, Marston's Pedigree, Wadsworth 6X and Wells Bombadier have all become 'Amber Ales' on their bottles and pump clips, while London Pride went from Best Bitter to the gloriously vague 'Original Ale', before finally landing on Amber in 2021.

The shift has left a lot of drinkers scratching their heads, but a quick look at the success of Sharp's Doom Bar might explain it. The ruby-coloured Cornish Bitter was first brewed in 1995 to local acclaim, and quickly spread throughout the UK. Stuart Howe, who was head brewer from 2002 to 2015, put that down to its very gentle bitterness and light body, which was more approachable to Lager drinkers and very adaptable to bottle. But it was also accompanied by some clever marketing. It made the name change from Bitter to Amber Ale around late 2005, and by 2013 was the biggest-selling cask and bottled real ale in the UK. With respect, few serious people would claim that Doom Bar is the best tasting Bitter in the UK, so along with the support of Molson Coors (who bought the brewery in 2011) its new title must have made some difference. Even if the name itself had little to do with it, it created a style that others wanted to be associated with.

To be fair, you can see why the marketing departments at other breweries might have followed suit. If you're new to beer, Bitter is not an enticing word. Humans are biologically disposed to dislike bitterness because it's a signal to our brains of potential poison. Most of us start to override the natural instinct to spit it out when we have our first taste of beer as teenagers, but the word still retains some power. Add to that the connotations of being a 'bitter' person, and you have an unhelpful bit of nomenclature.

Bitter is not even very accurate as a name either. The term was originally used to differentiate **hoppier brews** from sweeter, less-hopped Mild ales

By contrast, Amber Ale sounds soft and warming – two words I would associate with the style much more than bitter. Which leads us neatly to the fact that Bitter is not even very accurate as a name either. The term was originally used to differentiate hoppier brews from sweeter, less-hopped Mild ales of the 19th century. But today, Bitter is, in fact, pretty er ... mild. Where a modern version might be hopped to around 30 International Bittering Units – the measure used to determine the level of bitter hop acids in a beer – a modern West Coast Pale or IPA might be double that.

So while the style was originally named for its higher hopping rate, it only tells you a little about the beer. As we'll explore in this book around harvest time, British hops like Fuggles and Golding are vital components of traditional brewing. But only focusing on the bitterness does a disservice to two other ingredients that have equal importance in a Bitter's ultimate flavour: malt and yeast.

The malt bills of Bitters vary depending on where you are in the UK. Up in Manchester it's all about the pale Maris Otter malt, which brings a bright golden colour to beers like JW Lees Bitter (hanging on to the name there), as well as the bite of digestive biscuit and honey. In London you'll find more crystal malt and even a hint of chocolate malt, which are used in Fuller's London Pride to lend deeper notes of caramel and brown toast. Go further south and you'll find Harvey's Sussex Best, where the malt leads to a beer that verges on brown and is loaded with sticky toffee. But all these beers have an unexpected source of fruitiness on top of those characteristics.

Yeast is often overlooked when we talk about the aromas and flavours of British beer. We tend to presume that the sharper notes (like citrus, grass and bramble) come from the hops, while the richer ones (plums, caramel, bread) come from the malts. But actually a lot of them are created by the tiny microbe that knits it all together. For me, the defining joy of the Bitter is that backbone of residual ripe fruit that comes from fermentation.

For all the variation in hop and malt bills, real diversity can be found by focusing on Britain's house yeasts, many of which go back generations. Harvey's has used the same strain for over sixty years. Queen Elizabeth II had barely warmed up her throne when that original krausen was skimmed off the top of a fermenting beer and added to a second batch, and the process hasn't stopped since. Each time the yeast was used it absorbed a little of the beer's character, which has changed subtly thanks to sixty different hop and malt harvests and six decades of process refinements. The yeast would have shifted a little during the brewery's switch from copper to aluminium to steel vessels, for example – and while Harvey's mash tun is at least as old as the yeast, many parts have been replaced since. The yeast still holds

its secrets too – if you age a Harvey's Imperial Stout long enough you'll get notes of Brett, just like you would have with well-aged beer centuries ago.

When there isn't a fresh brew to add the yeast to, it's stored in chilled rooms in the cellar of the brewery, where it waits patiently to be used again. It rarely has to wait long, because all Harvey's beers are made with it. Head brewer Miles Jenner doesn't dare introduce any other strains for fear of either cross contaminating or even killing it – something he's come close to doing twice. The last time was in 2020, when COVID-19 forced him to stop brewing. Despite all the rents, wages and overheads he had to pay while selling virtually no beer, it was his yeast that Jenner was sure would drag his business under. 'I was looking at that bed of yeast and thinking if we lose it now, we go out of business. Our beer wouldn't taste the same again for a very long time.'

That's how central its flavour profile is to the beer, and how vital the endless cycle of cropping from one batch to the next is. Starting again with his insurance policy – a frozen sample at a yeast bank in Norwich years ago – would mean losing much of the nuance and character that yeast had developed.

For all his reliance on it, he's shy about saying exactly what his yeast adds. While beer writers like to break down beer into its constituent parts, the brewers know those parts inside out and are often more interested in the whole. Jenner loves the soft, part-baked dough note the yeast leaves in the malt, but on top of that I pick up ripe banana and apple skin too, especially in the Sussex Best.

Those aromas aren't just in the beer either, they're all around the brewery thanks to the fact that Jenner still ferments his beers in the open. Giving the yeast room to breathe encourages the yeast to produce stronger esters – the aromatic compounds that give those banana and apple flavours. But it also introduces an element of seasonality that closed, fully temperature controlled conicals remove. While the brewers can control the ambient temperatures, there is still a seasonal variation of Harvey's beers. Jenner says his Sussex Best is a little drier in summer, and maybe even more aromatic due to the temperature and speed at which it ferments. He embraces that, brewing bright and aromatic beers for Easter or summer, and stronger, sweeter beers like Tom Paine Ale and Christmas Ale in winter.

During the tastings that end Jenner's tours you can try four seasons in one day, but Sussex Best is the beer I always associate with the thaw days at the end of winter. The fresh dough and sticky toffee qualities are best paired with warm fires, steamy windows and mature cheese, but the fruitier yeast esters also hint at spring. They are like the sun breaking through a rain cloud to add contrast, and hint at the brighter moments to come.

Talking of moments to come, the term Bitter is not being committed to the past as yet. The craft beer revolution may have mostly started with ultra-pale, American-hopped beers but there is now a normcore trend forming, with many of the most celebrated producers releasing native styles. DEYA, Cloudwater and Five Points have all released English-hopped amber beers that are proudly labelled as Bitters. To see these brewers and their audiences enthusing about British hops and malts might mean that one day our regional brewers embrace the Bitter once again.

Fireside drinking

The right way to enjoy a warm pint

In the last chapter I was dismissive about the idea of British cask beer being served warm, but there is a darker side to enjoying a beer at around 10°C. While it definitely starts cool, real ale does get warm much quicker. We've all realised that in a midsummer beer garden, but it's also true when you snag the best seat in the house during winter. I'm referring, of course, to the stool by the fire.

It's there that I've let many a good pint go tepid while musing the great questions of life or googling the answers to a crossword. The direct heat from the crackling flames means I'm quickly down to a t-shirt, but you can't do the same for a beer, which can assume the temperature of a forgotten cup of tea within minutes. Thankfully, there are plenty of beer styles that are delicious at this temperature, and some are even better. Knowing which can ensure you still have a delicious pint half an hour later.

As you probably know through general life experience, coldness suppresses both flavour and aroma. When something edible is cold, the aromatic compounds become less volatile due to thermodynamics and the receptors on our tongues are less sensitive when in contact with them. It's why ice cream and Coca Cola are delicious cold but sickly when warm. The same principles apply to beer: most of its flavours are intensified as it warms up. Unfortunately, it isn't quite uniform, however, and some beers are thrown out of balance. A Helles can become sticky and dull, an American Pale Ale too bitter, and a Best Bitter cloying and lifeless. But academic studies have shown that sourness and saltiness don't tend to be perceived stronger at higher temperatures, and that the bigger a flavour is to start with, the less noticeable the change will be. That means there are plenty of styles that can stand the heat of the fireside seat – we just have to go big.

The most obvious style is Imperial Stout. Generally this style should be served at something approaching cellar temperature (12°C) anyway, because they are brewed to really come alive as they warm. Served cold these styles tend to express more of their roasted coffee and chocolate character, but the warmer they are the more the caramel and deep, dark fruits come to the fore. Just be wary of any Imperial Stouts with adjunct flavours, because such beers are often brewed a lot sweeter than traditional English-style versions. For me, the best Imperial Stouts in the UK are made by Siren Craft Brew, New Barns Brewery (the Plain Dark Beer is sensational), and Buxton Brewery, and I've enjoyed beers from them all at a fireside.

There are plenty of styles that can **stand the heat** of the fireside seat – we just have to go big

If you're looking for something malty but a little more session-strength, an English Brown Ale is a wonderful fireside beer. A good one is loaded with burnt toffee, golden toast and digestive biscuit, and those sweeter notes will grow as the beer warms, kept in check but never distracted from by a slightly lower hopping rate than you'd find in a Bitter. An American Brown Ale might work too, but they tend to be heavily bittered and too much when warmer. Finding the old-school versions is pretty hard, but Kernel makes some fantastic higher ABV ones, while Northern Monk Brew Co releases them seasonally – usually with a suitably northern name like 'We're From Yorkshire, People Are Sensible' – and defiant traditional brewers including Harvey's brew them regularly.

It would be tempting to get lost in the rural idyll of roaring fires and traditional British brewing, but malty styles aren't the only drinks that work. A Gueuze can be a

A Gueuze can be a **fantastic fireside beer** if you're looking for something fresher and zingier

fantastic fireside beer if you're looking for something fresher and zingier. Served at cellar temperature they have a more honeyed character (formed during the long mash and boil processes) that actually rounds out some of the acidity. You can also serve tart and tannin-heavy ciders, which are rounded out as the sweeter apple notes really open up. If you want a more hearty experience, a robust and heavily oaked cider really comes alive at the kind of temperature you'd serve a red wine. Both Oliver's Cider and Ross-on-Wye Cider revel in releasing whisky-aged ciders that taste like licking the barrel on the finish. That combination of raw but sweet oak with the smell of an open fire is as intoxicating as drinking gets.

The fact that more historic drinks suit warmer temperatures is no coincidence. It's worth remembering that in the days before refrigeration and central heating, all beers and ciders would have been served at the ambient temperatures of the seasons. On top of that, the UK's temperate (at best) climate means most drinking would have been done by the fire, or as close to it as you could get in a busy inn. Far from being bothered by warm beer, it seems our ancestors embraced it. Reading through recipe books and novels from the 19th century you frequently come across references to people heating up ale next to the fire or even using hot pokers to caramelise it. Most famously there's the Dog's Nose, mentioned in Charles Dicken's Pickwick Papers, which is a combination of warm Porter, gin, sugar and nutmeg, but more interestingly is a drink enjoyed both in the UK and its colder colonies – the Flip. This drink was made by whisking rum or brandy with eggs, sugar and spices such as nutmeg and ginger. The mixture was then combined with ale warmed by the fire and mixed by pouring between two jugs. The result was a smooth, eggnog-like cocktail that was then reheated using a red-hot poker, known as a 'loggerhead', from the fire.

Loggerheads are still used today to caramelise big beers like Bocks and Imperial Stouts, though usually as a bit of theatre at a festival or for a YouTube video. The effect is remarkable – the beer almost instantly boils to create a creamy head that foams right over the rim. The parts touched by the loggerhead caramelise to add a wonderful toasted marshmallow note, but unfortunately it does tend to knock the carbonation and life out of the beer, which is probably why our ancestors added such creamy, sweet and spicy mixtures to it as well. Still, if you own an open fire and are very curious and very careful, making a Flip or just a caramelised Bock is a very exciting way to set sparks flying on a dreary February evening.

National Pizza Day

Best served with cold beer

If there was ever a month that needed a Bank Holiday, or national event, or something – anything – to break up the monotony, it's February. Instead we're left with the cleaning-up job that follows Pancake Day and unnecessary pressures of Valentine's Day.

Perhaps that's why February has an unbelievable amount of National Something Days – dates picked seemingly at random, by no one in particular, to celebrate a specific thing. Things kick off cool with Baked Alaska Day on the 1st, warm up for Valentine's day with Shower With a Friend Day (5 February), and get heart-warming with Random Act of Kindness Day (17 February). I swear these are all official events with global recognition, but they all pale in comparison to one of the greatest days of the year: International Pizza Day (9 February). Valentine's can do one, because once beer is added to the equation, this is the true day of romance in February.

There is actually a specific Beer and Pizza Day (9 October for those who want to celebrate both), but October is one of the most abundant and exciting months of the year. February really needs this, and a pizza night at home is a wonderful way to spend a gloomy evening because it's a real social affair: mixing the dough, preparing the toppings and putting it all together. If you want to eat out, you'll be pleased to know that pizza has become a bit of a pub special, not just because it's quick to prepare and popular but because it goes so damn well with beer.

To demonstrate why, we need to start by being honest about what pizza is: an open sandwich. To those who just spat out their IPA, please let me point you to history. The first breads ever made – and we're talking around 9,000 years ago – were not really risen. They were flat, like chapatis, and usually topped with different ingredients and eaten by hand. Around 600 BC Persian soldiers baked bready disks on their shields and topped them with dates and cheese; the Ancient Greeks topped baked flatbreads with cheese, onion and garlic; and a little later in Rome, bakers topped their slightly risen focaccias with all sorts of seasonal produce. These were all precursors to the pizza, and my point is that they are all sandwiches – hand-held, bread-based vehicles for delicious ingredients.

Now, as any sandwich aficionado will tell you, it's the bread that matters most. You can have the most incredible fillings and toppings, but if they're laid on a slab of cheap white bread then it's going to be unsatisfying (an exception is made for sausage sarnies and bacon butties). The dough is by far the most important and tricky part of making great pizza, as well as being the element that changes most as you travel around the world. In Naples, the home of what we now consider pizza, the dough is chewy and nutty around the edge but floppy and tangy underneath – so much so that the only way to keep the toppings on is to flip the apex inwards on itself. But drive 150 miles up the coast to Rome and the base is thin and crispy, almost like toast. Over in New York, the giant slices are crispy too, and stand to attention when you hold them by the thick, airy crust. Try the same thing with a Chicago deep dish, however, and you'll get a cascade of tomato and melted cheese all over you as the flaky, buttery dough sags under the weight of toppings. As you can probably tell, the type of dough is going to be key to what beer pairing is best.

The origins of bread and beer are intertwined. The story goes that beer was invented when some enterprising young Sumerians decided to eat a baker's spent grain. Being moist and a few days old, it had begun to naturally ferment, creating alcohol and giving the Sumerians an unexpected buzz. We know this because of an ancient Sumerian tablet that depicts several people sucking at a bowl of grain with straws, and as far as humanity was concerned that was it. We advanced quickly from there – with nomads settling in verdant fields to sow and harvest grain, early engineers making pots and perfecting the art of brewing – and indeed regressed as we spent increasing amounts of our lives either a little drunk or a little hungover.

While most bread is now made with wheat (due to its high protein), and beer with barley (because of its easily accessible sugars), there are flavours in common across the board. The wild yeasts that make a sourdough starter are the same as the wild yeasts and bacteria that make our wild ales – that lemony tang is the same in both products.

It has **the bite of roasted malt,** but also some **berry sweetness** to match the tomato and **a little salinity** to pair with the cheese

It's only recently that UK restaurants have really started to explore all the different doughs, and it's opened up a whole world of beer and pizza matching, so long as you stick to the fundamental rule: there has to be some malt depth to the beer. Our beloved New England IPAs will do fine, but they will never enhance the experience – their oaty base is too light, and the sweet juiciness of the yeast and hops too bold. We also need some bite, but where it comes from will depend on the pizza you're matching with. It could be a tickle of prickly hops, the dry roastiness of chocolate malt, or even the snap of something sour; it just has to have a finish on it to compete with the simple but big flavours of great pizza.

When it comes to the classic Neapolitan, an Italian Pilsner is best. You might be surprised to hear that the wine-loving nation of Italy actually prefers to drink beer with its pizza. They believe that the carbonation helps digest the heavy dough, and it's the kind of food that needs plenty of liquid to wash it down – a dangerous game with wine. Italian Pilsner is a pseudo-style made famous by Birraficio Italiano Tipopils. It takes the dry, honeyed German Pilsner and

dry-hops the hell out of it with grassy and lemony European hops. The beer itself is often so hoppy you get a little haze, and a really tangy, dry and almost powdery finish that leaves you gasping for another sip. It cuts right through the doughy Neapolitan base, but is filled out by the acidity of the tomato and creamy mozzarella. If that's not to your liking, a lower-ABV Porter can be a great match too. It has the bite of roasted malt, but also some berry sweetness to match the tomato and a little salinity to pair with the cheese. Just be careful with the dough, as you can enhance the darker, acrid parts of the crust that catch in the oven.

If you're eating a Roman-style pizza, something a little sweeter is needed. A West Coast Pale Ale can add some of the bready depth that the thin crust lacks, and that citrusy hoppiness is dynamite with rich mozzarella and the cured Italian meats or anchovies that might grace the top. Italy has seen a craft beer revolution to rival the UK's, and there are some fantastic American-inspired brewers in the country. In both Rome and Naples you'll often find at least one American Pale Ale on the drinks list.

Roman pizzerias also have a penchant for the Pizza Bianco, or white pizza. Traditionally, they are just plain pizza bases, salted, oiled and herbed, that apparently started as little testers for the heat of the oven. They're eaten as street food, but are also great crispy bar snacks. The term is also used for pizzas that substitute the tomato sauce for a bechamel one. These affronts to proper pizza are then topped with more unusual things like potato and rosemary, and more common things like smoked meat. Whatever the topping, the creaminess needs acidity, so it's the perfect opportunity to bring out a simple, lemony Berliner Weisse, or if there are some aged meats or cheeses involved, a Flemish Red to add fruitiness.

Heading over to the other great home of pizza, New York, we need a slightly different approach. Here the dough is much thicker but still crispy, and usually big on the toppings in both variation and quantity. The classic pepperoni begs for a bold, caramel and pine-tinged West Coast IPA, but to be a little more wintery, a Black IPA can also work wonders too. This misunderstood style isn't really about the roasted malt that gives it the colour, it's more about the crystal and caramalt that adds sweet depth and body. Combined with some cutting, piney hops, it's absolutely perfect with an oily double pepperoni New York pizza.

I know I said pizza is a sandwich, but Chicago deep dish is more like a pie. The dough is made with a high proportion of fat to bind it and provide the structure it needs to form sides. As a result, it's drier and almost short (like pastry) so it needs something quenching and refreshing. At the same time, though, it needs to be a massive beer, because there is also a lot of oil, rich cheese, thick tomato sauce and probably a lot of Parmesan going on. For me, a Märzen or Bock are the best beers for such a slice – served by the pint and drunk at lightning speed, but loaded with everything from digestive biscuit to honeyed fig notes before a snappy Lager finish.

If any city should be enjoying its eponymous dish with German-style Lagers, it's Chicago. Throughout the second half of the 19th century thousands of Germans migrated there, bringing their bar culture and love of beer with them. Unnerved by the influx, in 1855 nationalistic mayor Levi Boon closed all the city's bars on Sundays and raised the cost of a liquor licence from $50 to $300. It was a cynical and targeted move against the German population, who traditionally worked six days a week and therefore socialised in saloons on Sundays. Over 200 Germans were arrested for flouting the new rules, and the resulting demonstrations were nicknamed The Lager Beer Riots. Tragically, one protestor was killed in the scuffle, but the licence fee was dropped to $100. A year later, protesters joined forces with Irish immigrants, and the $50 licence was restored.

Of course, the Chicago deep dish pizza wasn't around in 1855. Most of it's Italian immigrants arrived from between 1880 and 1920, and the deep dish was invented a few decades later. But it's interesting to note how the melting pot of cultures could lead to such serendipity of flavour. Like all the great love stories, it seems that even through adversity, Lager and pizza were clearly meant to be together.

Beer pancakes

Crisper, lighter, more flavourful

When I first started experimenting with beer in cooking, I had one very simple approach: if a recipe called for wine, water or milk, I tried it with beer. Obviously I gave it a little thought, picking the styles according to their acidity, malt character and strength, but the one rule I learned quickly was to never use anything hoppy.

I had some spectacular failures in the early days (the less we talk about the Milk Stout bechamel the better) but also some revelations. The first of them was this fail-safe recipe for pancakes, inspired by Jamie Oliver's one-cup recipe. Pancake Day is a risky enough occasion already, but adding beer to the batter required no reworking whatsoever. Not only is it almost impossible to get wrong, it's actually significantly better than any milk-based pancake I have ever had. The carbonation helps ensure a fluffy pancake, while the remaining sugar in the beer catches on the pan, meaning a glorious crispy edge to one side of every pancake you make.

It's also a super flexible recipe. In this version I've used Saison, cinnamon and blueberries, but they could all be subbed out for your own favourites. Porter and blackberry; Dubbel and raisin; Berliner Weisse and thyme? Whatever you choose, I suggest the American combo of crispy smoked bacon and maple syrup on top.

INGREDIENTS

(serves 2)

6 rashers smoked streaky bacon

1 mug of self-raising flour, sifted

1 heaped teaspoon ground cinnamon

1 large free-range egg

330ml ice cold Saison (not mixed ferm or hoppy!)

A few knobs of butter

200g fresh blueberries

Maple syrup

METHOD

1 Line a baking tray with baking paper, then lay the bacon on top. Put it in the oven, turn it on to 180°C and leave for 20 mins.

2 Meanwhile, get a large non-stick pan on a medium heat. Sift the flour into a large bowl, add the cinnamon and a pinch of salt, then crack in the egg. Tip in the beer and whisk until smooth.

3 Throw a knob of butter into the pan and let it melt as you move it around. Add a ladleful of batter and let it naturally form a 6-in roundel, then quickly scatter a handful of blueberries over it. Leave until the entire surface has bubbles forming over it – around 90 secs – then flip to cook for another 90 secs.

4 Repeat until all the batter is used up, putting the pancakes somewhere to keep warm. You should have six at the end, which can take some time so don't forget about the bacon! When it's ready, remove from the oven to some kitchen paper to soak up the residual fat.

5 Serve the pancakes in a stack, topped with the crispy bacon and a (un)healthy drizzle of maple syrup.

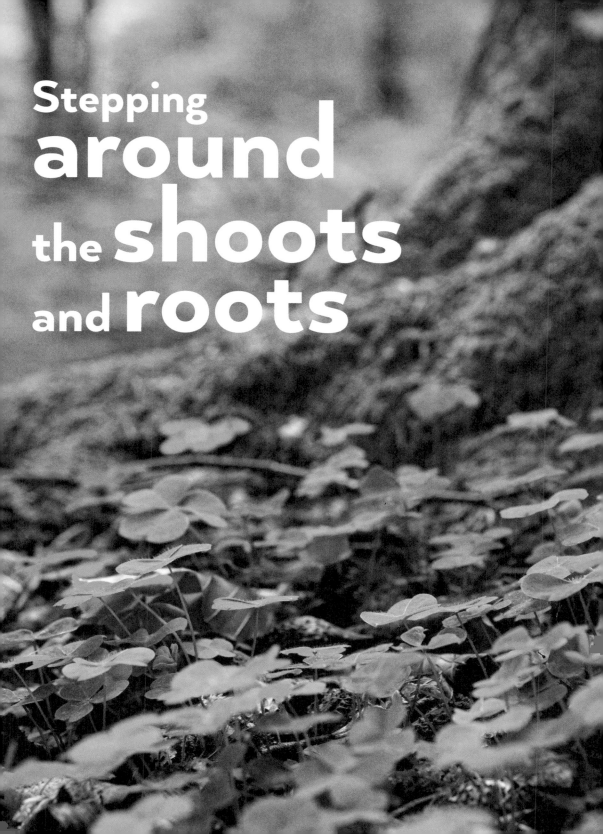

Stepping **around** the **shoots** and **roots**

March

March is the official start of spring, and an important month in the history of beer. As the world around us wakes from hibernation we're surrounded by the colourful sights and sounds of new life, including delicious early season vegetables and, of course, lamb – though that life is often cut rather short in the name of the Sunday Roast. This traditional meal has become synonymous with the British pub and historic beer styles like Porter, which sees a spike in sales along with Stout thanks to St Patrick's Day.

While the Irish national holiday is famous for drinking, the month of March is actually more about brewing. Today most breweries make beer all year round, some barely noticing the shift in seasons. But before refrigeration they would have all stopped for the summer, making the first few months of the year all about brewing enough beer to make it through to autumn. While some of that was laid down to age, most drinkers preferred fresh beer and there was only so much breweries could store. That put a lot of pressure on March. In fact, it was such an important time for brewing that one German Lager style was named after the month: Märzen.

In terms of actual drinking, despite Lent spanning most of March, there was probably even more than usual.

Apparently there's nothing in the Bible that says fasting included alcohol, and beer was often used as a liquid lunch by those not eating during the day. The most famous subscribers to this frankly dangerous way of life were the Trappist monks of Belgium. They typically brewed stronger beers to sell to the public (which was how they funded the monastery) and made a smaller beer for themselves. The small beers are almost exclusively available at the official cafés nearby, but the stronger beers are found all over the world, and as we'll learn, are ripe for ageing or drinking fresh.

What to drink

For me, this time of year is all about the Porter and Bitter, two styles perfect for that transition from the fireside, to windows bathed in sunlight, and then to the breezy beer garden. They are also the perfect accompaniment to the food of early spring, especially roasted lamb, where their malt character mingles with the gamey meat, rich gravy and sweet roasted vegetables. It would be remiss not to indulge in some Stout (even Imperial Stout) in the month of St Patrick's Day, too. Go independent if you can, as the UK and Ireland itself are blessed with great nitro-poured Stouts at this time of year – try those from The White Hag, O'Hara's, Titanic and Siren.

What to eat

Asparagus is in season and about to peak, and eating British asparagus is a revelation compared to the woody imported ones we get the rest of the year. Wild garlic is also everywhere and easy to identify even for those who have never foraged before – add it to chicken pot pies, or mayonnaise for the perfect asparagus dip (and have it with a clean, zippy Berliner Weisse). Otherwise, get the oven hot for some roasties and a beef joint or a leg of lamb (and add garlic and rosemary to both).

Where to go

Guinness has done an incredible job of making St Patrick's Day mostly about Stout, and who are we to argue? You can hunt down the official beer, but you'll also find pubs and bottleshops stocking all the seasonal dark beers that come out as a nod to the Patron Saint, so you don't have to fight your way through a crowded Irish bar to get a pint of the good stuff.

   Let's not forget that March also features Orval day. All good craft and Belgian-themed bars will put something together for it, whether it's a vertical tasting or limited stock of Abbaye D'Orval cheese (which is the best Trappist cheese). I also highly suggest buying a few bottles for home about nine months in advance.

This time of year is all about **Porter and Bitter,** two styles perfect for that transition from the fireside, to windows bathed in sunlight, and then to the breezy beer garden

St Patrick's Day

And the history of Porter and Stout

The biggest beer event in March, for better or for worse, is St Patrick's Day. On average, an incredible 13 million pints of Guinness are drunk in Ireland on that day alone – about three per adult. But anyone claiming that the day has lost its meaning and is now simply about getting drunk should remember that it's probably always been that way.

St Patrick is credited with bringing Christianity to Ireland, an event considered so important that the Church declared a feast day right in the middle of Lent. The rest, as they say, is history. You can't make a whole population fast for several weeks, then provide endless alcohol and food for 24 hours and not expect people to overindulge. Today, the food element is significantly diminished, so it's lucky for society in general that Guinness is only 4.3%. If it were the strength of Stouts in the 1800s, St Patrick's Day would be an annual riot. That's because Stout was originally a very strong beer, and its roots are not found in Dublin, or even Ireland, but in London.

Considering the style – if we can call it a style – was named after the city and its most vital workers, traces of London Porter are quite hard to find in the capital. On a cold and blustery March afternoon I set out to visit all the historic places associated with it, but tragically most of them have disappeared.

That might go some way to explain why the history of Porter is so confusing. It starts in the early 1700s, when British brewers were producing a more limited range of styles than today. Back then, beer was taxed on the ingredients rather than the final strength, so brewers tended to use very cheap brown malts for most of their beer. They also had less control over fermentation so they sold beer super fresh, before wild yeasts would turn them funky or even sour. These young beers were referred to as 'Mild', and made up most of what people drank in the inns of James II and Queen Anne's England. Those who wanted a bit more complexity could buy what was known as 'Stale', which was the same beer aged until some wilder character started to appear. That happened thanks to Brettanomyces (a yeast that added a scrumpy cider note) and potentially bacteria like Lactobacillus (which added lemon sourness). Both would consume the remaining sugar to leave the beer drier and thinner, so sometimes people would order a blend of Mild and Stale to get the best of both worlds.

Now, stale was a more expensive drink, and some entrepreneurial beer retailers realised that rather than buying stale beer from the brewers, they could just buy mild ale and age it themselves, and thus pocket the profits. Understandably, this didn't go down well with the mild brown beer brewers, who were also being hit with big tax rises on the malt they used. In response, the larger brewers decided to brew a new beer that circumvented the mild and stale issue. They took their brown beer recipe and reduced how much malt was going in, as well as switching that malt out for cheaper but therefore smokier varieties. Because the beer was lower in strength it needed more hops to protect it from infection, as well as longer maturation time to reduce the smoky notes. Doing so was a double win for brewers. Not only did they pay less tax and cut out any crafty maturation by the middle man, but they also created the demand for Stout Porter. These special, stronger versions were made with the first runnings – and sometimes only runnings – of the mash, so were a stronger or 'stouter' batch.

Who conceived this plan first is up for debate, but the fact that Parsons Brewery of St Katherine's in London bought a set of huge 130-barrel vats in 1713 implies they intended to age considerably more beer on site very early indeed. Wherever it came from, this longer-matured, hoppier brown ale went down a storm with the working classes. It was particularly popular with the street and river porters – effectively the Addison Lee drivers of olde England – who lived and worked in the shadows of the breweries. The long oak maturation and higher hopping rate created wonderful, unexpected flavours that would have been a perfect beer for their physical outdoor work: despite being cheap, London Porters would have been around 6%, and sweet, roasty and robust with it. The porters were so well known for drinking the beer that it was even named after them, which, according to beer historian Martyn Cornell, appeared in print for the first time in 1721.

Porter went on to become the UK's most popular beer for over a century, and was exported to India in considerably greater volumes than India Pale Ale ever was. In fact, there was a time when the style was so popular it made Truman's Brewery on Brick Lane the biggest in the world.

But you wouldn't know that to look at the breweries and pubs of London today. Aside from Fuller's and Five Points, the style is mostly overlooked by the city's breweries, and even the architecture seems to have erased it. The name Porter Street and a plaque is all that is left of the original Anchor Brewery site of Barclay Perkins, and there was nothing around Parsons Brewery in St Katharine's Dock. Despite hours of searching in East London I could find only one pub that still advertised Porter in its historic stone hoardings. That's probably because most of the capital's pubs were renovated at the very end of the 19th century, just as Porter was losing market share to other styles. In a bid to premiumise it, Stout took its place on the signs next to a combination of Ale, Pale Ale or Mild – the latter had reinvented itself as lightly hopped and sweet dark ale. I did, however, find Porter adorning The Lord Clyde, a beautiful early 20th-century Truman's pub just a short walk from the old Barclay Perkins brewery. And you don't have to travel far to find another wonderful relic of the Porter age: Porter and oysters.

In the 1800s oysters were incredibly cheap. It's an often repeated statistic that in 1864 London alone consumed over 700 million oysters – roughly 230 per person. They were sold as street food, used as cheap meat in pies, and of course sold in all manner of ways in the inns of London, alongside Porter and Stout. Despite being so overfished it has become an expensive speciality, oysters and dark beer is still a

Oysters and dark beer is still a **niche part of our culture.** It's also one of the highlights of visiting Borough Market

niche part of our culture. It's also one of the highlights of visiting Borough Market, especially around this time of year when native UK oysters are in season but it's warm enough to sit out. Porter makes a brilliant pairing with the salty and slightly buttery crustaceans – the salinity really brings out the fruity malt sweetness. For the ultimate experience squeeze a lemon and (or) a drop of hot sauce over it, and enjoy on the topsy-turvy poser tables outside Wright Brothers Porter & Oyster House.

Oysters and Porter (or Stout) are such natural partners that they are even brewed together. Oyster Stout is now a style made by a small subset of brewers, including Hammerton Brewing in North London. Founder Lee Hammerton decided to open a brewery long before he knew that his grandfather had owned one, only finding out when he told his mother the plan. It turns out that the original Hammerton Brewery was well known for its Oyster Stout, and Lee decided he had to make one, even if most people wrinkle their nose at the idea. Pentonville Stout started as a core beer, but as tastes have got a little sweeter in beer it's become a seasonal.

For what it's worth I think it's Hammerton's best beer – it's gorgeously rich and roasty with a definite hint of salt that makes it extremely moreish. The name is slightly misleading, you'll be relieved to hear. No actual oysters go into the beer, only

their shells, which are added to the boil so they are well sanitised. There they add a little minerality, but more importantly help clarify the beer, which is most likely why they ended up there in the first place. If you're wondering who on earth thought of adding them, remember there were 700 million shells piling up in the streets of London. Finding a place for them must have been high on everyone's agenda.

So this explains the history of Porter and the rise of Stout in its place, but it doesn't quite explain how Stout became a session-strength, smooth beer in Ireland. The story starts in 1817 with the invention of Black Patent malt. Until that point Porters had been brewed almost exclusively with brown malt, which didn't have much fermentable sugar but gave Porter its dark colour and smoky, roasty flavour. The invention of black malt allowed brewers to use the more efficient pale malt alongside a tiny addition of black to produce a cheaper, less smoky, but still very dark beer.

In London most brewers retained a little brown malt for decades to keep the beer closer to its original flavour, but in Ireland, where Porter was also very popular, most breweries stopped brewing with it entirely. One of the breweries to make that switch would have been Dublin's Arthur Guinness & Sons, which sold its first Porter in 1778. Guinness was an absolute powerhouse of a brewery in Ireland, rivalling some of the bigger London businesses by the late 1800s before Porter finally started to go into decline. That was when the brewery's first great innovation helped it survive and set it apart: advertising. The work of artist John Gilroy in the early 20th century, coupled with the spurious tagline 'Guinness is Good For You', was the brewery's first step towards becoming the brand we know today.

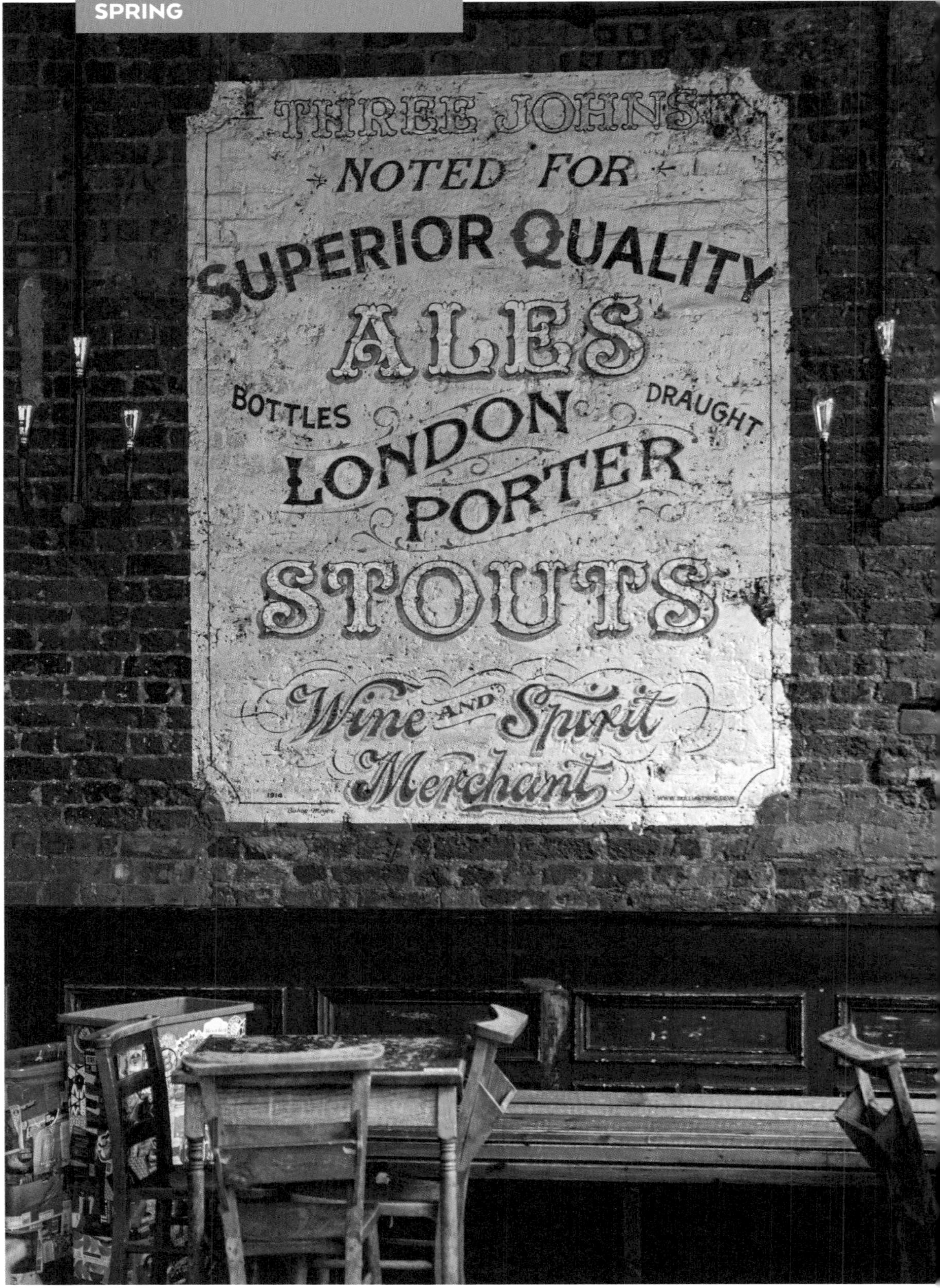
THREE JOHNS
NOTED FOR
SUPERIOR QUALITY
ALES
BOTTLES
DRAUGHT
LONDON
PORTER
STOUTS
Wine AND Spirit
Merchant

Modern Porters make a great match with **some of the seasonal produce coming out** – just try it with griddled asparagus and a squeeze of lemon

Still, the Porters and Stouts it was brewing conformed to the original definitions: both used black malt and one was stronger version of the other. In the 1950s, though, the brewery decided to bump up the attenuation of its beer – the amount of sugar consumed during fermentation. That meant they could either make stronger beer (which they charged more for) or liquor it back to make more beer from the same amount of grain, saving them money. Either way the result would have been a drier and slightly thinner beer.

Guinness was also famously lively and over-carbonated, requiring publicans to pour the beer between jugs to knock some of the bubbles out before pouring into the glass. Even after that they had to pour the beer in two stages to ensure it didn't froth over the top. This resulted in a thick and creamy head that would have helped add body to the lighter beer underneath. The brewery took that one step further in 1959 when it started pouring the beer using nitrogen. Nitro or 'smooth' pouring would have given the beer the same creamy head, but would have also made the beer underneath incredibly soft and silky, thanks to the smaller bubbles and the fact that nitrogen doesn't have the carbonic acid tang of CO_2.

The change in attenuation and pouring method were the genesis of the Irish Dry Stout as we know it: dry, loaded with burnt toast and dark chocolate notes, and as smooth as velvet. Guinness was unlike anything else in the world at the time.

Thanks to similarities in look and flavour, the eventual pervasiveness of Guinness's Irish Dry Stout meant Porters and Stouts came to be seen as essentially the same thing. Where they have aligned in ABV, they have diverged ever so slightly in flavour, with Stouts typically being drier, with more roasted coffee and dark chocolate character, while Porters retain a little more biscuit and fruity character that could have been part of the brown beers of old. For me, modern Porters are a great autumn and winter style, because they smell of frothy coffee and poached fruits, and make a great match with some of the seasonal produce coming out – just try it with griddled asparagus and a squeeze of lemon. Meanwhile Stout (mad as it sounds) is a little crispier and at session strength can actually be a refreshing summer drink, which might be part of why it's so popular in West Africa and the Caribbean.

Stout's ownership of St Patrick's Day is a great example of how humans have created their own seasonality. Nothing in nature could really predict the volume of dark beer consumed in March, and therefore the amount of it made in January and February to prepare. Given how unfashionable session-strength dark beer has become, it serves as an important reminder to beer lovers and passing St Patrick's Day revellers how delicious and easy drinking they can be.

Time makes great beer

But fools of us all

March was once a strange and hectic time to be a brewery. Just as nature sprang from the earth with new life and colour, brewers started laying things down for months of hibernation.

In the days before refrigeration, production pretty much stopped over the summer in most parts of the world because the souring bacteria that could spoil a young beer thrived at warmer temperatures. That made September and October the busiest time of year. Not only did they have to buy and process that year's hop and barley harvest, they had to refill their stores and customer's cellars with beer after months of not brewing. On top of that, they were also taking advantage of the seven months of cool temperatures ahead – ideal for maturing some strong beers. These aptly named 'October Beers' often aged out to way beyond 10% ABV by the time they were drunk the next autumn, and were the early ancestors of what we now call Barley Wine (we'll talk more about them in the autumn chapters).

The summer hiatus meant March was nearly as busy. Even if there was no harvest to deal with, brewers needed to mash in enough beer to make it through the summer. Some of it would have been drunk within a month or two of brewing, but the rest had to last up to six months, and that gave rise to some very special beers indeed. Like October beer, the most famous of these also took their names from the season it was brewed – namely the Märzen and the Bock.

The Märzen is a rich, dark-copper Lager that originated in Munich and has a vital place in brewing history. The Bavarians had taken the summer break a step further than most regions, with its young ruler, Duke Albrecht V, officially outlawing brewing between St George's day (23 April) and St Michael's Day (29 September) in 1553. Clearly Albrecht didn't subscribe to the core belief of my youth – that bad beer was better than no beer.

So if Bavarians wanted enough beer to make it through to autumn that meant a lot of batches being brewed in the new year. For three centuries most of that beer would have been a dark, malty and smoky beer called Braunbier, fermented by the naturally occurring Lager yeasts that were native to the region. At this time of year they were brewed stronger and hoppier to see out the summer in cool caves below the city, like those hewn into the Nockherberg below the original Paulaner Brewery. There's a lineage between these 'Sommerbiers' and the dark, liquorice-like beers we know as Doppelbocks today – many of which are adorned with the spring image of a baby goat (which is Bock in German).

These Sommerbiers would have been served at the public celebration of the marriage between Bavarian King Ludwig I and Princess Therese of Saxe-Hildburghausen in 1810, on a field just outside the city. It must have been quite the party because there's been a one held there nearly every year since. In fact, it's the

biggest beer festival in the world: Oktoberfest.

As the tradition grew, it became a very important source of income to the breweries of Munich (and it still is). In a bid to get one over on its rivals, Spaten Brewery decided to brew an entirely new beer for the occasion, unveiling the first-ever Märzen beer at the 1841 festival. Like Sommerbier, it was brewed around March with lots of hops and lagered over the summer, but Spaten had used kilning techniques developed in England to produce a beer several shades paler. It would have had less roastiness and smokiness, and more of the biscuit and honey we associate with modern Lager. We'll learn more about the impact of this in the summer chapters.

The Märzen was revolutionary back then, but it's a rare beer style these days, with only a handful of German brewers still making them. Once Spaten's head brewer, Gabriel Sedlmeyer, and his friend, Anton Dreher, had brought the British malting techniques back to Central Europe, it spread and evolved quickly. Dreher took it back to his Schwechater brewery in Austria to brew what has become known as the first Vienna Lager, and other Munich brewers started using it too – including Josef Groll, who took the idea to Pilsner when he became head brewer of the newly formed Pilsner Urquell in 1842. His beer is heralded as the first Pilsner, and Lagers

have only turned paler as tastes changed and technology improved. Oktoberfest today serves a modern version of the Märzen called Festbier, which was invented around 100 years later. It's more golden and slightly less hopped to suit the palates of 20th-century drinkers, but still carries a caramel hint from a higher ABV and richer malt.

Temperature control and better understanding about yeast means macrobreweries can now produce Lager-like beers in a matter of days. But while capitalism encouraged some breweries to shrink brewing and maturing time, others still recognise the importance of letting nature run its course. Although we now don't need to store our beers for so long, or ferment them in open vessels, many continue to. Time is still a vital ingredient in the brewing of great Lager.

The reason is that Lager yeasts prefer to work at roughly 8°C, so the fermentation and maturation steps happen at around half the speed of an ale yeast. If fermented too warm or not matured fully, undesirable flavours such as diacetyl (a butterscotch note), sulphur and acetaldehyde (apple skin or even nailpolish in high doses) could appear. Despite also battling with heavy roasted flavours and notes of smokiness from the malting process, 19th-century brewers would have been well aware that low temperatures suited their beers best.

But brewing slow and low isn't only about avoiding off flavours. 'Lagering', as cold maturation has come to be called, also seems to add something to a beer. Explaining what is difficult, but it's something like a clean minerality and snap on the finish. All well-lagered beers share this characteristic, whether it's the Imperial Stout-inspired Baltic Porter or double decocted Bohemian Pilsner. Perhaps it's not that the process adds flavours, more that lagering makes a beer so clean that flavours that would otherwise be disguised come to the fore. How long that takes depends on the beer's recipe, the specific yeast, and the temperature it's lagered at, so it can vary from just four weeks to a whole year. For the brewers of Märzen, around six months was good enough to make Munich and Oktoberfest one of the most famous beer destinations in the world.

The irony is that as soon as these matured beers are packaged and sent out, they are best drunk fresh. The delicate flavours that lagering reveals can get hidden again by the ravages of time outside of dark and cold tanks. Oxidation adds cardboard and caramel, while lightstriking (caused by UV light) can add a weedy note, both of which will ruin the clean snap of a Pale Lager. That's increasingly important as the weather improves and we start to think about crystal-clear, pure golden pints of frothy Pilsner. March occasionally graces us with a day or two of beer garden weather, and we can pretend the summer is nearly upon us for a few glorious hours.

The irony is that as soon as these matured beers are packaged and sent out, they **are best drunk fresh**

Orval Day

Some things get better with age

It's not just Lager that is best drunk fresh – pretty much all beers are. While anything over roughly 7% has the potential to improve in bottle, there are so many variables that it's usually not worth the risk. Remember, the brewery released it when it did for a reason.

There is, however, a very small selection of beers that might just keep maturing. Lower-hopped beers turn cardboardy a lot slower, darker beers can carry those oxidised sherry notes better, and beers with wild yeasts tend to develop further, but one precise rule I stick to is that anything you want to age beyond the expiry date should be bottle conditioned.

This is the process of naturally carbonating a beer by dosing the bottle with sugar and (or) yeast, then leaving it to referment at warm temperatures. The carbon dioxide created goes into solution under pressure in the sealed bottle, with the amount dictated by how much sugar was left to ferment. The initial process only takes a matter of weeks, and it's used widely for bottled British Bitters and Belgian ales that are delicious fresh. But for some beers and yeasts, leaving it to condition longer can have a wonderful effect on the flavour.

The Trappist breweries of Belgium, that is to say monasteries whose monks produce their own beer to fund their way of life, are famous for the slow processes they use to make their beers – something enabled by the lack of commercial pressure. Westmalle Brewery lagers its Tripel for weeks, then bottle conditions for months on end before releasing it; Chimay puts its world-famous Grand Reserve Dubbel in 750ml bottles because they believe it ages better that way; and Rochefort puts five-year expiries on all its beers. The most remarkable bottle-conditioned Trappist beer, however, is Orval.

Late March sees the international (but still very niche) celebration of Orval Day. It comes a few weeks after this special Trappist brewery announces that year's 'Ambassaduers' of Orval: those pubs and bars that show enough commitment to the beer to become official representatives. Perhaps the day is meant to celebrate them, but I like to think it's because the weather is warming and all over Europe the Brettanomyces yeast in every bottle of Orval is coming to life.

Abbaye D'Orval has centuries of history, but the brewery and the beer we know today were created in the 1930s. The monastery was destroyed by the French in 1793, but the foundation stone of a new abbey wasn't laid until 1929, with a brewery being added two years later to help fund reconstruction. At the time it was owned and supported entirely by local lay people, which helped the brewery hit the ground running, despite (or perhaps because of) the eccentricities of brewmaster Martin Pappenheimer and technical manager Jan van Heule. Heule had spent a lot of time in England and even owned a brewery of his own in Ostend, where he

made classic British styles like Porter and Pale Ale. He brought the British methods of infusion mashing and dry hopping to Orval's beer – extremely modern techniques when compared to Pappenheimer's antiquated brewing philosophy. Most notably, Pappenheimer refused to clean his open fermenters too thoroughly, either thinking it made no difference or believing that a Brettanomyces infection would be a welcome part of the monastery's terroir. It gave the original Orval beer a very dry, fruity and funky flavour that, to Pappenheimer's credit, seems to have been popular.

Pappenheimer died in 1942 and by 1949 there was no one left in the brewery with sufficient brewing expertise, so two young monks, Brother Dominique and

Father Raphael, were sent to Scourmont Abbey – known to beer geeks as Chimay – to learn to brew. Along with advisers from outside the abbey, they revamped the entire brewing set up, and in doing so started brewing uninfected, but much less tasty beer. The story goes that Brother Dominique scoured the whole brewery in search of something carrying the original Brett yeast to add to the beer – presumably organic, porous things like wood – until he managed to recreate the character.

That strain is now added at the bottling stage of the process, rather than during the first fermentation. Like most Trappist beers, Orval undergoes a long bottle-conditioning period before being sold, but when fresh from the brewery that Brett character is still pretty mild. In fact, the beer is sweet and sherbety, with lovely fresh orange pith notes and marmalade bitterness from the hops. Because Brett is a slower-acting yeast than most standard brewing strains, the real fun begins about six months later. It's at this point that the farmyard, scrumpy cider character starts to kick in and the beer turns dry. For me, anywhere from here to a year is Orval at its best. It comes climbing out of the bottle to greet you, is so effervescent it seems to pop on your tongue, and it's the perfect combination of hoppy pale and wild ale.

After about 12 months another process begins. By this age the Brett has eaten all the remaining sugar and the beer is probably a little higher than the stated 6.2%. As a result, the remaining oxygen, or any seeping into the bottle via the cap seal, isn't being eaten up by the refermentation. And so Orval starts to age in a more traditional way: by oxidising. Like in all beers, oxidation suppresses hop character, adds a light caramel to the malty tones, and eventually brings a sherry-like note to the beer. This can work nicely with Orval's pithy, zesty character, but it can also be overdone – though it depends on your personal tastes. The most fun you can have with Orval is to try a vertical of several different ages – ideally fresh, one year, and three years old. Many Orval Ambassadors will do something like this for their Orval Day event, and the best places will get in some Trappist cheese to go with it.

I tend to buy six or so bottles every March to ensure I have a range of ages to call upon if I'm not in a pub on the big day. Working out which age is your favourite is a rite of passage for a beer geek, and I'm often asked how old I like mine. The brewery puts a five-year cellaring date on it, but I wouldn't let it go past three. It rarely goes undrunk that long in my house anyway.

It comes climbing out of the bottle to greet you, is so effervescent **it seems to pop on your tongue,** and it's the perfect combination of hoppy pale and wild ale

The pub roast

As British as the beer we serve it with

There was a time in Britain, a brilliant and bizarre time, when we drank beer with every single meal. I'm not just talking about the adults either – the kids joined us in supping small or table beer at breakfast, lunch and dinner until the late 1800s.

The main reason was that beer was safer to store and drink than some water sources, and was also believed – to some extent correctly – to be nutritious. It was so much a part of our diet that schools even had breweries and the posher ones had dedicated 'beer butlers' to serve it.

Even after we snatched pints away from our crying newborns and studying teens, beer and food were inseparable whether you were the queen or the ploughman. Workers in the fields started their day with a mouthful of bread, cheese and beer, while royalty were likely to finish their day with the same. In between there would have been beer with every meal, and one particular pairing comes up in every historical record you care to check.

Beef and ale is more than a pie filling, it is the stodge upon which our nation was built. It sustained the workers and satiated the rulers, was found at the most humble of luncheons and the most significant of celebrations, and everything in between.

Given that ale was safer to drink than water (and the cow population probably rivalled the human one back in the 1800s) it's pretty unremarkable that these two foods were seen every day, but the fact that they still formed the basis of our celebrations just shows how much the British loved them both. Beef and beer – most likely Porter – was the traditional Christmas meal for centuries, as well as the feast at the coming of age celebrations, and the workhouse parties thrown by usually exploitative masters. Despite consuming this combination day after day, and associating them with horrendous working conditions and long hours, we could still think of nothing better to eat and drink than beef and beer. Over 100 years later, I have to agree.

When the gastropub became a thing it was immediately vilified by the people who love pubs most – beer drinkers. But anyone who thinks this was some new-fangled, capitalist bastardisation of the British pub needs to pick up a history book. Pubs are not just about beer, or any drink for that matter. The main purpose of the pub has always been a place to rest, meet and eat. Beer only came into the equation because it was inseparable from the food.

The renewed focus on pub kitchens has mostly been a bid for survival. Within the current climate, a pub is only really profitable for the person who owns the building. Profit margins on beer itself are so wafer thin that those who run them, especially those in the tied estates who are required to buy some or most of their beer from their brewery owners, rely on sales of food and wine to actually pay themselves a wage. The only benefit of this situation – and one so outweighed by

the negatives I feel bad even making this link – is that the quality of Sunday roasts in pubs has dramatically improved in the last two decades.

Maybe it's because I'm British, maybe it's because I was brought up by a home economist, or maybe it's because I believe that the roast potato is the greatest single human invention, but for me the Sunday roast is the ultimate meal. At home it's as close as we come as a nation to a true sharing table like the Italians do so well, while in the pub it has become a focal point for the gathering of friends and family too. The casual, homely feel of a good pub means it will always be a more natural place for a roast than a restaurant. But I think the main reason we love a pub roast is the fact that there's good beer there.

Porter still makes a wonderful match with a modern roast dinner. As we've discussed, Porter was a strong, well-matured dark beer made from brown malt. Today the old-fashioned and inefficient brown malt has been replaced with lots of biscuity pale, caramalt and crystal malt, with a small addition of roastier dark grain. The result is a beer with notes of brown toast, milk chocolate and fruits like figs and dates that match beautifully with rich gravies, roasted vegetables and charred meats. Porter is fantastic with beef but it's also brilliant with lamb, which is of course in season in March and April. Its umami-like gaminess (which comes from the fat) can clash with a lot of flavours, but the dark fruits and brown toast of a Porter really complement it, and happen to go brilliantly with many of the classic seasonings added to roast lamb: rosemary, garlic and even mint. Porter isn't perfect for everything though, and can be a little heavy for chicken and not sweet enough for pork. For those meats we need something different from the bar.

Luckily, the classic British Bitter is a wonderful match for chicken and pork. Even the paler varieties will still carry some of that caramel (or perhaps honey) flavour, with some fleshy fruit character coming from the yeasts to match the sweetness on the plate. In fact, since they were brought up together in the same house, pretty much all British styles of beer will go with your roast dinner. Stout, Mild, Golden Ale, even Barley Wine if you're not intending to do anything else for the rest of the day. The only real rule is that it should be from the cask pumps (though there is an exception to be made at Christmas, as we'll learn). The combination of low carbonation, cellar temperature, caramelised malts and residually sweet British yeasts are just the perfect partners to a roast and are almost extensions of the gravy. All that really has to be avoided is American hops, where citrus fruits and robust bitterness can really distract and overwhelm what is already a pretty complex mash of flavours.

So while we may moan when all the tables are taken and the aisles crowded with pushchairs, it's worth remembering that not only is Sunday one of the most important days for the pub's takings, it's also a beautiful moment that brings families and old friends together – some of whom may live such busy lives that it takes such events to give them the time and peace they need to connect. Centuries ago it brought them together regardless of class and social standing, and if Sunday roasts keep that ideal going then the gastropub was a great idea after all.

Porter-roasted brisket

History in a pot

A roast dinner is a personal thing. It's not so much what goes on the plate, but how we cook it. To many of us it's a ritual and everyone has their own, so I won't use this book to impose mine on you (even if I do think only heretics boil carrots and fools don't rub their chicken with butter, garlic purée, fresh rosemary and smoked salt). What I'll do instead is tell you the absolute best Sunday one-pot wonder.

Roasts are intense, sweaty affairs. Every time I start one I tell myself this time will be different. I will get my timings right and coast casually towards the finish, carving up just as the roasties crisp, the gravy thickens and the guests sit down. In reality, I run a relay between kitchen and table, cursing in between giant gulps of beer. The one-pot roast avoids all those difficulties, combining the meat and gravy into one process and being forgiving enough to just wait for the rest of the meal to

finish. This recipe also requires opening two beers, but not necessarily using the entire second bottle, which means the chef gets their reward.

It's inspired by a meal I had on my honeymoon, at the Rising Sun pub in Truro, Cornwall. I say I had it but really my wife ordered it. I just happened to eat the lion's share because it was just about the most delicious thing I'd ever tasted. The beef pulled apart like warm bread, and the gravy was as rich and comforting as vegetable soup.

You can adapt this version to your tastes or the seasons, but the fundamentals are always the same and dead simple. There are two main ingredients, and they are the same ingredients that make up the perfect Sunday – beer and some time to relax.

The reason it's perfect for this time of year is that the traditionally heavy beef can play host and friend to all kinds of beautiful early spring vegetables. For me it's like a last blast of winter, before spring and summer eating really begins, or that last fireside beer before we all go into the garden.

INGREDIENTS

400g rolled beef brisket

1 large onion, diced

2 carrots, diced

1 celery stick, diced

4 cloves garlic, peeled and halved

1 tbsp of tomato purée (or better a handful of cherry tomatoes, halved, if in season)

Sprig of rosemary

Sprig of thyme

Worcestershire sauce

Either 2 x 500ml or 3 x 330ml bottles of Porter (as unhoppy as possible)

1 Savoy cabbage

METHOD

1 Pre-heat your oven to 140°C. Put a thick-bottomed stew pot on a high heat and add a glug of olive oil.

2 Brown the beef on all sides until golden and crusty, then remove to a plate.

3 Lower the heat to medium and add the onion, carrots and celery, and fry for 15 mins until golden and soft, stirring often.

4 Toss in the tomatoes, garlic and herbs, then season well with salt and pepper.

5 Fry for another 10 mins then place the beef on top. Pour in half the Porter and a hearty shake of Worcestershire sauce and bring to the boil.

6 Cook in the oven for about 4 hrs, topping up to make sure the beef is always covered. If you run out of beer or drink the rest, switch to water.

7 With an hour to go add the cabbage and top up one last time.

8 Remove from the oven when the cabbage is cooked and the sauce is thick and unctuous. Take out the sprigs (if they survived) then pull the beef with a fork and stir it all together.

9 Serve over buttery mash with griddled purple sprouting broccoli or British asparagus with a squeeze of lemon.

Finding
refreshment
in **endless**
showers

April

April is the beginning of beer garden season. Whether that's a picnic table and a cask ale at your local, or a stubby lager in the rain while stubbornly tending a barbecue, everything we drink is now influenced by being outside rather than sheltering inside.

German Maibocks were brewed to celebrate this exact moment (though the moment has slightly shifted into April due to climate change), while Belgian Easter beers give religious folk a reward at the end of Lent (and everyone else just another excuse to have a beer). Strangely – or perhaps because they evolved at very different times to each other – few beers brewed during or for this time of year match the ungodly amount of chocolate we now eat thanks to Easter eggs. Easter beers tend to be blond and pretty hoppy (neither of which are ideal for sweet food), and another seasonal style that definitely won't go with chocolate is IPA.

April happens to be the most exciting time for British-brewed American beers. While we can now store our hops cold and safe all year around, it's still noticeable when really fresh hops are used, and this is the time of year that the latest American hop harvest lands on our shores. Expect a glut of amazing IPAs from excitable brewers who can't wait to tell us how catty Simcoe is this year, or just how juicy this crop of Azacca smells. I suggest humouring them, because the IPAs are likely to be better than at any other time of year.

What to drink

Now is the best time to drink IPA – the hops are fresh off the boat from America and you might even be able to enjoy it outside. All the beers made with the new crop should sing louder than ever (look out for a reference to the latest harvest on the can), but some breweries release their biggest IPAs at this time of year. Cloudwater releases special editions that celebrate their favourites from the fresh bales, and Magic Rock has been getting beer geek's hearts thumping with its annual Human and Unhuman Cannonball launches for nearly a decade.

If you're more into Belgian Blond Ales or strong German Lager then this is also a great season for you – spring sees the release of De Dolle-inspired Easter beers and historic Maibocks. Most breweries who excel at Lagers or Belgian ales will at least make something that nods to these two great traditions.

What to eat

Given that most Easter Sundays fall in April, the answer is probably chocolate, but you also might be hosting the first barbecues of the year, for which I heartily recommend tossing some new season potatoes with garlic, olive oil and rosemary then roasting (yes, roasting) them to make mini jacket potatoes. On the colder days when we have to retreat indoors you can add a hint of spring with a rhubarb crumble – served with a Milk Stout or fruited Berliner Weisse.

What to do

Dodge the showers and get down to the local beer garden to enjoy something blond and ideally American hopped – it will still be cool enough for cask outside, but we're now getting into keg season, which is usually served a few degrees cooler. With the glut of IPAs coming out you can also head to Northern Monk's Hop City, a weekend-long celebration of our lovely brewing flowers. There are usually fringe events in the centre of Leeds, but you don't really need an excuse to check out North Brewing's Springwell brewery and taproom.

Now is the **best time to drink IPA** – the hops are fresh off the boat from America and you **might even be able to** enjoy it outside

American hops

Why IPAs might taste best right now

In the introduction of this book I talked about how globalisation has created a new form of seasonality – one still based on the seasons, but influenced by human actions and culture. In no part of the brewing scene is that more obvious than in our use of hops. Despite growing throughout the temperate latitudes of both hemispheres, brewers all over the globe have chosen to rely on one harvest – that of north-west America.

For breweries in the region, that means new hop deliveries from October – it even means fresh hop beers like we have in the UK in September. But breweries further away have to wait months for the hops to be dried, processed, packaged and shipped across the globe. In the UK the biggest and best customers might start to see varieties arriving from January, but the deliveries start in earnest in March and April. That makes this time of year one of the most important for those who focus on modern American brewing. The quality and character of those hops will define what they brew, how they brew and the flavour of their beer for the next year.

It's a much heard refrain among beer lovers that some beer or another is 'not the beer it used to be'. It's a criticism levelled at pretty much any brand that has more than a few years of history, and I used to write off such statements as anecdotal and unfair. But I've come to realise there is a lot of truth to it, just not the truth those beer lovers intended. You see, no beer is what it used to be. It's not always the brewer dumbing things down for financial gain or to cater to less discerning drinkers, as many are accused of doing. It's usually because the hops and malt that went into it (and probably the water and yeast too) are quite literally not what they used to be. They are agricultural products that change with the seasons and the years, and the brewer can either embrace it like a wine maker does, or shift the recipe to account for it. We rarely talk about beer in terms of vintages, but there is a good argument that we should. With such reliance on that one American hop harvest, there is a global shift in beer every year, and the variation in character and indeed quality in hops can be pretty wide.

That means getting hold of the most popular varieties is famously competitive. Most are sold through just a handful of distributors and cooperatives, who, understandably, focus on their bigger and more high profile customers. Those breweries will have contracts going forward years for specific quantities, while the

We rarely talk about beer **in terms of vintages,** but there is a good argument that we should

10KG CHINOOK
10KG CHINOOK
CRYO

rest of the industry orders as and when they need them. There's nothing wrong with buying 'on spec', but there are advantages to having hop contracts beyond simply peace of mind.

Much like grapes, there is a real sense of terroir to hops. The states of Oregon, Washington and Idaho account for 97% of hops grown in the US, a country that produces 40% of the world's hops. That's partly because their climate is able to produce the kinds of hops that modern breweries want – they all have mild and wet springs, bright and warm summers, and the perfect soil. That means the hops grow quickly and abundantly, then ripen fully on the bine. But even within the region there is variation from state to state, farm to farm and field to field – all down to groundwater run-off, the aspect of the land, the microclimates, and the times they were picked. That means certain rows of bines develop subtly different aromas and flavours – and some brewers are able to select their hops from the exact field they prefer, choosing certain characteristics to suit the vision they have for their beer. One of those lucky breweries is Manchester's Cloudwater Brew Co.

Cloudwater was an early part of the second wave of British craft breweries, and unlike the former homebrewers who set up with makeshift old dairy tanks in dilapidated railway arches, it was well funded. Through a combination of founder Paul Jones's forward-thinking and (then) head brewer James Campbell's experience,

Some brewers are able to **select their hops from the exact field they prefer,** choosing certain characteristics to suit **the vision they have for their beer**

they hit the ground harder and faster than any brewery before them. They were voted the fifth best brewery in the world by the users of RateBeer in 2016, barely 18 months after opening. Since then it has been regarded as one of the most important brewers in the world, and was offered space at the American hop selections during harvest very early on.

Whether it's the process of brewing or political and charitable causes, Cloudwater has always used its beers and marketing as an opportunity to educate. The original concept was a season-based brewery, releasing quarterly collections of styles that suited the time of year. For the reasons we discussed in the introduction to this book, that didn't work commercially. Still, the brewery has clung on to several seasonal elements and one of those is a series of beers focused on new hop harvests. Each year the brewery releases a series of beers with the same malt, yeast and water profile but puts a fresh hop variety front and centre. In 2020 – which used the 2019 harvest – they released 14 one-off IPAs that started with the classic orangey notes of Amarillo (in a beer called Fresh Cut Climbing Frame), and moved through juicy

Citra, pithy Idaho 7, coconut-y Sabro and tropical El Dorado. Each was markedly different in aroma, flavour and even texture, to the ones that came before.

The interesting thing about hop selection, though, is that what one variety smells like in whole cone or pellet form is often very different to how it will appear in the final beer. The presentation of Citra when used in the boil is very different to being used in the whirlpool, or during an early, warm dry hop, or a very late and cold dry hop. Brewers doing hop selections are presented with several different 'lots' of fields from which they can narrow down what they want to buy, but in doing so they have to look at the potential as much as the immediate impression. Lots of dank, resiny aroma may make it super compelling in pellet form, but will that mean too much savouriness if used to dry hop? Or if a brewer's house yeast is already exceptionally peachy, is it a good idea to pick a lot that also has loads of stone fruit and may make a one-dimensional beer? Paul has to make his selections right there at the table in the US about his brewing plans for the next year back home.

That makes Cloudwater's 'Crop Year' beer series an exciting moment for drinkers, as we see the direction the brewery's beers will take. We get to learn that at the same time as the brewers, who smell and taste for the first time what their hops will give them for this vintage and how they need to adapt their recipes of planned styles.

Clearly, hop selection isn't just about getting the best hop – it's about getting the best hops for your brewery. What Paul loves most about being able to select his is what he calls 'the luxury of straying from the norm'. Simcoe is one of the most popular hops in American brewing because its mix of pithiness and citrus makes it a brilliant counterpoint in Hazy IPAs, while its dankness and slight caramel sweetness makes it a natural partner in West Coast IPAs. But selection allows Paul to drill down into the

Because they're unpasteurised and often extremley hoppy, **most craft beers are suprisingly delicate.** They can spoil in a matter of days

differences between the different lots and find something extra that will be unique to his beers. As a result, he no longer buys Simcoe from its original home in Yakima, Washington, but from a farm in Idaho, where to him the Simcoe has a pineapple note on top of the pine and dankness. Perhaps it was the power of suggestion, but I could see what he meant when we rubbed some pellets between our hands.

Another way in which Cloudwater has used beer to educate the drinker is through an obsession with freshness. Because they're usually unpasteurised and often extremely hoppy, most craft beers are surprisingly delicate. They can spoil in a matter of days in the presence of oxygen, a matter of hours at warm temperatures, and a matter of seconds in direct sunlight. Most breweries will rightly tell you to keep your beer in the fridge, but not all of them make sure they are refrigerated even on their way to you. So-called 'cold-chain distribution' is the norm in the US, but over here it's less common. Cloudwater endeavour to work exclusively with distributors who can guarantee cold transport, and encourage all their retailers to store their beer in fridges even when not on sale.

It's understandable given the planning and processing that goes into each new release, and it would be a shame for drinkers to let all that good work go to waste at the last moment. There is a lot of hand-wringing in craft beer around the idea of drinking fresh, and a lot of it goes so far that people pass on beers only a few weeks old. In reality, it's not the time that's so important, but the temperature. A well-made New England IPA that has been kept in a fridge its whole life will taste brewery-fresh for about three months, but one kept out of the fridge will develop stale flavours within a week. If there was ever any proof of this, look at the fact that the hops being brewed with at this time of year will still be delicious come next spring if kept cold. Conversely, drinking a beer that was only packaged a matter of days ago isn't always a great idea – hoppy beers can come across as harsh and savoury, while others can suffer from a little-understood affliction called 'bottle shock', which mutes the bigger flavours of the beer for up to a few weeks. So while we should celebrate freshness, we should never fetishise it.

Of course, Cloudwater aren't alone in celebrating freshness and the arrival of the new American hop harvest. While not many breweries release 14 different IPAs, plenty release special beers that show American hops at their best. Collaborations between breweries and their hop suppliers have become common, particularly where the supplier is hoping to launch a new variety, product, or raise the profile of a specific farm it works with. There isn't a better time to go deep on hoppy beer and explore the world of hop-saturated brewing – and next time you say a beer isn't what it used to be, you can say so with a smile, and a toast to nature.

Easter beer

As fresh as a spring shower

Some beer styles are easy to define. They may have coalesced over decades (or even centuries), but today we can be pretty specific about how they should be put together. We know the colour (recorded as SRM), bitterness (through IBU) and sweetness (via FG). We can expect hops from related countries, specific malts to make a minimum proportion of the grist, and the use of certain yeasts. Even if we don't know all that, we innately understand what a Pilsner should taste and look like, just as we do an American IPA.

But some styles are more difficult to pin down. They are more like concepts, defined as much by what they're not as what they are. Everyone has a slightly different idea of what a Black IPA should be, for example, which is one of the reasons the style faded into obscurity around 2015. But the most nebulous beer style, or should I say concept, that I've ever come across is the Easter beer.

It's quite possible you've never even heard of it, but I can assure that within a tiny niche of European-inspired breweries it's very much a thing. Before you get excited, though, don't expect the level of investment in kitsch and excess you get at Christmas. Both styles are a reflection of the time that inspired them. Christmas beer is all about boozy warmth, heady spice and roasty flavours. In other words, it's about decadence. Easter beer is more thoughtful. The religious versions were, of course, celebratory – it denotes the end of Lent and a toast to the resurrection – but increasingly, Easter beers have become more an expression of the season. As a result, the style blends into the even more loosely defined spring beer, found all over Europe and now the world. Historically, that would have meant different flavours in every country, region and brewery, but modern springtime beers have at least started to fall into two camps: the German and the Belgian.

The German side of the family is much easier to understand. The nation's Maibocks (Mai means 'May') started as lower-strength versions of Doppelbocks – the very strong, hoppy dark Lagers first brewed by the Paulaner monks of Munich and consumed as liquid bread during Lent. Doppelbocks are still celebrated during 'Starkbierfest', a frankly dangerous indoor version of Oktoberfest where 8% beers are served in litres and you make friends for life that you can't remember come morning. Maibock season follows shortly afterwards, and until the 1800s the beers would have been dark too. It's thought that the colour started to lighten because Maibocks bridged the gap between the dark, wintery beers and the lighter, summer ones. Indeed, the Maibock is traditionally seen as the beer served when the beer gardens of Bavaria start to open up in April and May. Today, they are sometimes referred to as Helles Bocks, because they are even lighter than standard Bock beers. They have the bright crispness of a Helles, but a lovely sweet caramel note (think Caramac bar) to them that complements the floral quality of the German hops.

While a Lager of this strength and drinkability would cause most drinkers to fall off their barstools, there are some wonderful examples being made in the UK. My picks at this time of year would be from Braybrooke in Market Harborough and Utopian from Crediton, Devon.

So far, so simple. But when we cross the border into Belgium things get confusing very quickly. There's Passbier, Bière de Pâques, Bière de Mars and Bière de Printemps – and these closely related styles bring in elements of lagering, lambic mashing and Trappist yeasts, as well as brewing traditions from nearby France and even some English brewing processes, too.

The best place to start is with the two breweries and beers that beer lovers claim to be the origin of modern Belgian Easter beer. Slaghmuylder's Paasbier (Flemish for Easter beer) is a hoppy, golden Pilsner with a fresh grass and rich malt notes. For me, that brings it a little too close to Maibock territory to claim to be its own thing. But the other seminal Belgian Easter beer comes from a very different perspective, and a brewery whose name literally translates 'The Mad Brewers'.

De Dolle Brouwers has a pretty good claim to making the first modern Easter ale. First brewed in the early 1980s, De Dolle Boskeun is less refined but infinitely more complex than Slaghmuylder's. If Passbier is a recently mowed lawn, the boozy, blond Boskeun is a wild meadow. Its chaotic floral notes, grain character and fruity esters combine to create berry, acacia, jasmine and even vanilla notes.

These incredible characteristics have caught the imagination of Belgian-focused breweries all over the world, most of whom would reference Boskeun if asked about their Easter brews. Generally these beers are blond and pretty strong – around what I call the 'baiting' strength, where you think you can have a couple of them then realise you definitely can't – with plenty of doughy brioche, honey and digestive biscuit malt character. Most will have big estery yeast profiles of clove, banana and pear, but a few breweries have used peachy English-style strains, too. Either way they should add big, intoxicating aromas that play with a high hopping rate – the keen sting of spring nettles and dewy grass are vital to making this beer feel vibrant and wild, like an April shower. It's for this reason that no Easter beer should really be aged. It should feel fresh and new, so ageing this character out not only means losing that wonderful hop aroma but also severing any link to the sights, sounds and flavours that inspired the brew.

One brewery that really understands this is The Brewery of St Mars of the Desert, which despite the name is found in a small industrial estate in Sheffield. Co-founders Dann Paquette and Martha Simpson-Holley have a deep reverence for Belgian beer, and especially De Dolle. The branding has the same hand-drawn, child-like vibe, and the brewhouses themselves have things in common, too. Most notably, both still use a coolship. While neither makes spontaneous beer, they seem to enjoy both the tradition of this cooling method and the element of risk that using it entails. Both breweries make bold, yeast-forward beers where a little unintended mixed fermentation would only add complexity and intrigue. In addition, the fact they never know for sure that they are making 'clean' beer leaves a little of the magic in the process.

There is plenty of magic in St Mars's Easter beer, Fluffy White Rabbits. It's made with lots of wheat for a pillowy body and two heady Belgian yeasts (one of which is a Trappist strain), as well as being whirlpooled with kilograms of floral, spicy Strisselspalt and Ekuanot. The use of such an American hop may seem incongruous, but it presents red berries and orange peel rather than all-out tropical notes. It also adds plenty of bitterness to the Goldings used in the boil, another thing it has in common with Boskeun. The result is a remarkably full-bodied and velvety beer, with enough hop character to be labelled an IPA if it weren't for the wave of banana and clove esters. With its nourishing bready notes and rasping, addictive bitterness I can't think of a better reward for forty days of Lent, nor a more dangerous one: in true tradition, it should be enjoyed with a hearty meal.

In case you're starting to think you understand modern Easter beer, I'm afraid I have to muddy the waters a little. You see, the Belgians have several springtime beers that predate Boskeun and Passbier. First up is Bière de Mars ('March beers'), which were made towards the end of the spontaneous season by doing a second (or

The keen sting of **spring nettles and dewy grass** are vital to making this beer feel **vibrant and wild,** like an April shower. It's for this reason that no Easter beer should really be aged

even third) running through the turbid mash to create a low-strength and refreshing young Lambic for the summer. Given that most European breweries were making stronger beer to keep through the hotter months, this shows how much Lambic brewers leaned into the idea of funky, sour beer.

The rise of Pilsner is probably responsible for this tradition dying out in the early 20th century, but the name Bière de Mars then got swallowed up into the entirely different brewing culture of Bière de Garde ('keeping beer') and its sub-style Bière de Printemps ('Spring beer'). These Northern French styles were strong beers made to last through the summer, like the German Märzen. Because of the local yeasts and ingredients, however, they would have presented much like a farmhouse-style Saison does today – albeit with some stale character thanks to the longer ageing. In modern brewing the lines between these styles, sub-styles and concepts are completely blurred. Breweries all over the world brew beers under these names, but can't seem to agree which is which. All I can do is tell you about the beers I've tried and what you might be able to expect from the beers that carry these diverse names.

Bière de Garde and Bière de Printemps tend to be Saison-like, with plenty of spice from the yeast, a rustic grain body and restrained hop character. Traditionally, they would be well aged and even show signs of wild yeasts, but breweries tend to release them young for drinkers to age themselves. It's worth noting that some breweries will use the word Printemps simply to show their intention to make a beer that's inspired by spring (and perhaps Belgian brewing) without buying into the style's history. Burning Sky's Saison Printemps is a straw-coloured, dry-hopped Saison at a very 'garden tinnie' strength of 4.2%, while a few Printemps beers are also made with classic spring ingredients like elderflower.

It seems that modern Bière de Mars is close to De Dolle's idea of Easter ale, but with less hoppy freshness and more malt depth to make it well suited to breezy, chillier early spring. St Mars's Bière de Mars is a deep amber, bittersweet and aromatic beer that has a slight banoffee vibe with the freshness of lemony hops. If you've ever had Palm Speciale, it's like a richer and more alluring version of that.

This is all anecdotal, of course. There isn't much literature around these styles and, much like Easter itself, the origins are being lost under the weight of new traditions and commercial pressures. Even if that's the case, I still love the intention behind these modern interpretations. Each one is an expression of how the brewer sees this beautiful season, and in a scene where the temptation is to brew what everyone else is brewing, that's an important new tradition to uphold.

Beer and chocolate

The best way to enjoy Easter eggs

I'm fairly certain they didn't celebrate the resurrection of Christ with chocolate, but I know for sure someone would have done with beer.

Easter Sunday is one of the few religious feast days we still celebrate in the UK, probably because we get the Monday to recover. Historically, we would have consumed beef and (more importantly) lots of ale, but the tradition of also giving eggs to children at the end of Lent has survived longer – aided by those real eggs being subbed for chocolate ones. Unfortunately, matching beer and chocolate is much trickier than beer and beef. In fact, matching beer with anything sweet is fraught with risk.

We've probably all had that moment where we're enjoying a beer with a main course: the sweet malt, soft carbonation and crisp, hop finish cleansing our palate perfectly. Perhaps there's a little beer leftover when you're done, or you ambitiously poured another pint mid-course. 'No problem, we've still got dessert to go,' you think. But then pudding arrives, you tuck in and take a hearty swig from your pint – and the beer turns to ash in your mouth. All the subtlety and the balance of the original is gone. Only bitterness remains.

I use this example as proof that beer and food matching is no marketing ploy or hubris. What we eat and drink matters deeply to how we perceive flavour – and there's a scientific reason for this. When we talk about tasting, we're really talking about two separate processes.

One happens in the nose, which is where we perceive what we'd call flavour: the gorgeous, aromatic things we crave like fried onions, freshly ground coffee, warm bread. The tongue doesn't get involved in any of that, despite what many people think. As well as helping with speech, our tongue is basically a life saving device, there to make sure we don't put anything poisonous in our bodies. It does that by detecting things that we need, and things that we definitely don't. Sugar and salt are things our bodies need (in moderation) so they are pleasant to us, while bitterness and sourness can be signs of poison so we react strongly to them. In fact, if you eat or drink something really bitter you can even get a flight-or-flight rush of adrenaline, like being on a rollercoaster. Some psychologists say this is why people get addicted to bitter and spicy flavours.

Chocolate, like beer has **a huge range of flavours:** white and milk chocolate can be incredibly sweet, while dark chocolate can be as bitter as burnt toast

Now, our body needs to be able to taste even tiny dilutions of toxins at all times. That means that when you eat something very sugary your sweetness receptors will retract a little to allow you to still process other tastes, which brings us back to that pint you had with pudding. The sugar means your ability to taste sweetness has been diminished, so when you take that sip of beer, you get none of the residual sugar that's balancing out the beer. All you get is the drier malt tones like coffee, toast and crackers, with the bitterness of the hops brought to the fore.

We need to take that into account when finding beers to match with dessert, looking for sweeter beers or those with decent acidity. It's why Imperial Stouts and fruited sours are the easiest to work with, but some traditional British Bitters and Belgian ales can really work at the end of a meal, too. That's because chocolate, like beer, has a huge range of flavours: white and milk chocolate can be incredibly sweet, while dark chocolate can be as bitter as burnt toast. That makes them brilliant partners as we match intensity across the spectrum, but it also means the chance of getting it entirely wrong is pretty high. One tip that should apply across all these matches is to serve the beer a little warmer than you would normally – that decreases the cognitive dissonance of temperature, but also increases the perceived sweetness of the beer.

White chocolate

When it comes to saccharine forms of chocolate, we need bold, strong and sweet beers. White chocolate goes brilliantly with Belgian strong ales – that spiced brioche kind of vibe matches the vanilla-y cocoa butter, while the esters of banana and pear can add lovely complexity. The high carbonation of Belgian beer also lifts the creamy texture. The best match I ever had was a Rococo cardamom-infused white chocolate with Duvel, but a Berliner Weisse with a fruit addition – particularly red berries – is a refreshing way to cleanse the palate after each square.

Milk chocolate

Milk chocolate is one of those treats that's so delicious it's hard to explain. Our love of it is universal, like pizza, burgers and Pilsner. But it's actually one of the hardest foods to find a beer match for.

Perhaps it's the sanctity of the flavour – some foods are just better on their own – or perhaps it's simply that the flavour is so intense, and its texture so palate-coating, that no other flavour can really get a look in. One thing is for certain, you need a lot of sweetness and a lot of body to have a hope of a match working. You can have a lot of fun matching it with massive, bold and adjunct-heavy Pastry Stouts, but they are essentially liquid chocolate anyway. Richer fruit beers can be delicious too, not citrusy ones but cherries, raspberries, figs, dates and raisins. Porters can also be fantastic if they're sweet enough, because the malts can bring cashew and other 'fruit and nut' notes.

Dark chocolate

For all my talk in this chapter about needing sweet beers, the roles are somewhat reversed when it comes to dark chocolate. Above 70% the balance starts to skew away from sweetness and creamy cocoa butter towards the cocoa, with its broody notes of dark berries and coffee. That means that the beers can be a little less syrupy, but they still need to retain some to balance out the bitterness.

Stouts and Porters aren't so helpful here. Sweeter ones might enhance the darker flavours, but most will just cancel each other out, like raindrops colliding. Here the best thing to do is to contrast the darkness with some colour, and to match the intensity through complexity. Kriek Lambics – spontaneous blended beers aged over cherry – create a gorgeous Black Forest Gateau vibe, while the style's sister, Framboise, adds a jammy tartness. Milk Stouts can add back in that creamy milk texture, and barrel-aged Imperial Stouts will add a liqueur-like alcohol heat, especially if the barrel is a powerful whisky or bourbon one. Is there a better way to finish a meal than a chocolate liqueur?

Nature
comes out of
hibernation

May

May was traditionally a quieter time for the brewing industry as the summer slowdown began in April. There's no such break for the farmers supplying the breweries though. At this time of year the last of the barley is sown while the first fields are just pushing through the earth, looking more like grass than grain.

Hop shoots are emerging as well, and the growers start the backbreaking work of wrapping the bines around their training wires so they grow upwards in lines. It's always done in a clockwise direction, otherwise they will unwrap themselves as they rotate to face the sun east to west each day.

With so much replanting and young growth happening, this time of year is sometimes referred to as the 'hunger gap' because nothing is ready to harvest. But out in the wild there is an abundance of nature ripe for picking. May is such an exciting month in the UK that there's even a brewery founded to celebrate it: May Provisions. This offshoot of Southampton's Unity Brewing makes an annual Saison celebrating spring produce, and while the timing of it isn't traditional (Saisons were historically made in winter and laid down until summer) May Provisions aren't the only ones who enjoy playing with the style come spring. There is lots of foraging and mixed fermentation happening as brewers seize upon what's local to make beers with a sense of place.

What to drink

Hopefully by now the beer gardens are in full swing and you're drinking prickly Golden Ales and Bitters, or crisp Pilsners or Helles on the really hot days. But certain Belgian ales can be wonderfully refreshing when served ice cold thanks to the high carbonation and bright spicy aromas – zesty Witbiers, Strong Ales and Saisons are all full of life. I love a great picnic with sharing bottles of beers like Yonder Annie, Lost and Grounded's Hophand Fallacy or anything pale by Little Earth Project.

What to eat

May doesn't bring a lot that's new to supermarkets – the seasonal vegetables and fruit are much the same as in April – but spring greens are in full flower. These are basically young, loosely packed cabbages, so they're perfect for frying off in butter with bacon and spices to serve next to barbecued or roasted veg and meat. If you're brave enough to forage, however, you'll find all sorts of exciting herbs and fruits coming out – elderflower, woodruff, wild strawberries, thyme, marjoram. You'll also find lots of fresh British mackerel appearing in your fishmongers, and they're brilliant on the barbecue.

What to do

We're teetering on the edge of festival season, but none seem to fall in May. Instead it's a great time to go camping because the countryside looks its best and the tents don't turn to ovens in the morning. There are some wonderful beer-focused places to camp, including Little Earth Project, Fyne Ales, Rivington Brewing Co, Batemans and more. If cider is your thing there is some fantastic glamping and camping to be found in the wilds of Herefordshire. You can even camp at Ross-On-Wye Cider and Perry Company's pub, the Yew Tree Inn.

Hopefully by now the beer gardens are in full swing and you're drinking **prickly Golden Ales and Bitters, or crisp Pilsners or Helles** on the really hot days

May Provisions

Brewing in times of abundance

Despite being the smaller side project, May Provisions is probably closer to what founder Jimmy Hatherly intended Unity Brewing to be.

When Jimmy started Unity in 2016, the idea was to bring Belgian brewing to the UK craft beer scene. Most of Jimmy's first beers were Saisons and Dubbels, inspired by lowland monastic or pastoral brewing and presented in beautiful 750ml sharing bottles. Even his house Pale Ale used a Belgian yeast and European hops, and was a pretty good homage to Brasserie de La Senne's legendary Taras Boulba.

However, in his own words, Jimmy was 'a little naïve'. British craft beer lovers were still obsessed with American hops, and couldn't quite get their palates round the spicy, floral nature of Belgian yeasts. So while there was a small audience of excitable beer lovers buying every release, he wasn't able to grow the sustainable business he wanted. And so he changed tack, rethinking his core range and introducing a more recent obsession – New England-style brewing.

In terms of flavour, the two worlds could not be further apart. Hazy IPAs provide intoxicating overripe stone fruit and hoppy citrus, but Belgian styles are more about heady spice and bready malt tones. For all their differences though, they share one very important characteristic that attracted Jimmy: both styles are heavily reliant on yeast. New England IPAs use old English strains selected for their sweet peachy esters, while most Belgian ales are brewed with strains that create notes of banana, clove, pear and apple skin. Despite the sensory difference, they both need similar care and attention from the brewer to reach their potential, and bold decisions to be made around pitching rates and temperatures.

With Jimmy's innate understanding of that, Unity came to be known as one of the UK's best IPA brewers, but this led to a new problem. Unity's new fans were picking up Unity's Belgian-inspired beers expecting delicious IPAs, and this made for some less than favourable Untappd reviews. Rather than wind down his Belgian brewing, Jimmy saw it as an opportunity to start again, launching a dedicated brand to provide an outlet for his love of the Lowlands.

While it always felt like he was holding back a little with Unity's Belgian ales, quite the opposite is true of May Provisions. He makes defiantly untrendy beer styles, uses heritage ingredients, and in the name has set a challenge in himself to

Hazy IPAs provide **intoxicating overripe stone fruit** and hoppy citrus, but Belgian styles are more about **heady spice** and bready malt tones

always think seasonally. With its beautiful, text-heavy labels and detailed descriptors, he knows that only those looking for such beers will be picking these off the shelves.

The Belgian Pale Ale was one of the first beers brought back. Now called Extra, it's even drier and spicier with an oily, floral and nectar-like aroma. He has also brewed a British-style IPA, made with heritage malt and all UK hops. It's legitimately bitter and marmalade-like, but it has a distinct mixed-fermentation feel thanks to some Saison-like spice and banana. Traditionally, it would have been more likely to show some Brett character, but the joy of mixed fermentation is letting nature make those kind of decisions for you.

From there, however, things get significantly wilder. Jimmy's background is in wine, which means he has an affinity with grapes and barrels. He describes his Saison aged in Sauvignon Blanc wine barrels as the beer he's been 'building towards' all this time, and when I visited there was a steel vat filled with Belgian Wit ageing over the skins of Reisling grapes from a nearby vineyard – supposedly the only Reisling grapes in the UK. It tasted like a fresh sip of that distinct wine variety, with jasmine, fresh melon and apple skin flavours, and tannins cut through by waves of gentle acidity.

While most of the beers seem to be inspired by historic recipes and also wine, seasonality unpins it all. Jimmy named the side project after the abundance of less traditional brewing ingredients that are available at this time of year, and in May he always brews a Saison that celebrates late spring. It was that brew day that I witnessed when I was last down. As I walked through the door, Jimmy was weighing out around 3.5kg of spruce tips – the new shoots that grow as the weather warms at the end of winter. Before they turn woody and firm up to extend the branches, spruce tips are soft and edible, loaded with sweet piney sap and citrus. They are

pretty tasty just eaten whole, but in a beer they mimic hops remarkably, albeit with a more woody edge rather than bitterness.

Brewing is all about process, and, importantly, being able to repeat it. So it's always enjoyable to see a brewing team trying something for the first time, referencing the same homebrew blogs and forums that I use, and debating the best way to do it on a large scale. After much back and forth on what, when and how much, the spruce was added in giant mesh bags as the beer cooled after boiling. As they were thrown in, out came a pouring of lemon-infused steam, tangy sweet and spa-like.

Weeks later, as I tried the beer for the first time, I was surprised by how subtle they were in the beer itself, lending a sappy freshness to the banana-y yeast, and adding a little pine note to the spiced, honeyed Goldings hops. The beer felt a little like the Easter beers of April, with lots of body and sweetness but seasonal hint of rain-soaked pine notes, reminding me of camping trips as a kid.

Technology has given brewers the freedom to brew beers that evoke an old memory, or that embed us in the exact time and place we're in. Jimmy has the immediacy of NEIPA – so all-consuming, accessible and modern – and the timelessness of traditional Belgian and British brewing. And thanks to the division of May Provisions and Unity, the drinkers know which one is in which can.

Foraged beer

The wildest kind of brewing

When you've driven three hours out of London – across the eerie plains of Salisbury and on through the rolling Mendips – to go foraging, the last thing you expect your expedition leader to do is take you straight to a leisure centre car park.

As we parked up I said as much to Stu Winstone, founder of Somerset's Yonder Brewing and Blending. Since it was a hot day, he suggested a quick dip might be welcome, but we'd come here for what was found behind the swimming pool.

Yonder is one of the UK's most experimental breweries. To some that term might conjure images of cryo hops, genetically modified yeasts and big, shiny machinery. But in an industry constantly looking for the new, sometimes the most innovative thing you can do is look to the past. Stu and his team do exactly that, using woodsman knowledge handed down over hundreds of generations and relying on wild yeasts and bacteria to make their beer. By putting foraging and wild fermentation at the heart of its beers, Yonder is one of the few remaining UK breweries that is entirely reliant on – or should I say inspired by – the seasons. Barely a week goes by that Stu isn't out in the Mendip Hills looking for ingredients to add to his beer and he knows all the best spots – including where to park, apparently.

We walked around the red brick building to find a hedge-lined cycle path, weather-worn and cracked where roots had forced their way through. At least, that's what I saw – Stu wasn't looking down, he was looking up and around, as if trying to track down the source of a noise I couldn't hear. Then he started pointing: there are sloes here, raspberry bushes behind that, wild strawberry coming through there and wild onions underneath. He grabs some nondescript stem and shoves what turns out to be marjoram under my nose, and I realise that this is no ordinary path. This is a larder, and there's one thing it is absolutely crammed with.

Once you know how to spot it, elderflower is everywhere in the UK. It's not that it's difficult to recognise – the beautiful white bouquets are unavoidable in late May

In an industry constantly looking for the new, sometimes the most innovative thing you can do **is look to the past.** Stu and his team do exactly that, using woodsman knowledge handed down over generations

and June – but foraging is a mindset that once you turn on becomes increasingly hard to turn off. Rather than just seeing generic hedgerows or fields, you start to break them down into constituent parts and discern what's edible. Unlike many of the things Stu gives me to try, you wouldn't actually want to eat elderflower. Traditionally it's used for cordial, but it's even better in beer. It has a gorgeous floral aroma that can work in everything from cask Golden Ales to wild Saisons. The stuff we were picking, however, was destined for a New England IPA.

Yonder doesn't really make American IPA. Stu and his team are passionate about British ingredients – the more local the better – and they have only broken their own rule because they are collaborating with one of the world's best producers of the style: DEYA Brewing Company. Foraging with us is DEYA head brewer Gareth Moore, who is clearly relishing a day not spent climbing in and out of his lauter tun. He still had an early start, however, because elderflower is best picked in the morning. The aroma is mostly in the pollen, and getting to the flowers before the insects do each morning can make all the difference. There's plenty of pollen in the flowers we take: they explode in a fine green powder every time we cut them from the stem. We take no more than a third from each bush, leaving a third for the plant and a third for the insects.

As we make our way down the path, we stop at several other plants that catch Stu's eye. Mostly he's making a mental note of where to return when the time is ripe, but every now and then he plucks something from the ground and gives it to us to try. Everywhere we look we find camomile, which looks exactly like a giant daisy. Rubbed between your fingers that honeyed aroma starts to come out, but it needs to be dried to really sing. The same isn't true for the wild thyme, oregano and marjoram we pick, which are pungent and herbal, and the ground ivy – a minty and sage-like herb that's dying to be put in a lamb kebab. We also collect a basketful

Foraged plants : **1** Wood Sorrel *(Oxalis acetosella)* **2** Chamomile (German). *(Matricaria chamomilla)* **3** Yarrow *(Achillea millefolium)* **4** Thyme *(Thymus polytrichus)* **5** Woodruff *(Galium odoratum)* **6** Marjoram *(Origanum vulgare)* **7** Elderflower *(Sambucus nigra)*

The use of **foraged and seasonal** ingredients in such modern beer might help beer geeks **re-establish that connection** between the beer we drink and the world around us

of woodruff, a pleasingly symmetrical, tall-stemmed plant that smells of vanilla and aniseed, particularly once dry. It's one of Stu's favourite herbs and has made it into several of his beers, including being the hero of a beautiful Saison a few years back that I hope will be brewed again one day.

It takes about two hours to collect enough elderflower for today's brew – roughly two hop boxes worth – and we then jump in the car. Back at the brewery, the elderflower is going into the whirlpool with a huge addition of aroma hops: hot enough to sterilise any wild bacteria but not hot enough to break down the aromatic compounds. There Stu and Gareth hope it will combine naturally with limey Motueka hops and passion fruit-tinged Strata. It's a very different process to Stu's usual approach with this spring flower, which would see it end up in wooden barrels or giant plastic containers of funky wild ale. There it would likely spend months infusing its flavour into the beer, before being released in autumn.

Because of the time between foraging for and actually releasing a beer, Stu usually has to assume it will be drunk at a very different time to what the flavours might suggest. But this IPA only needed a few weeks – and for the first time, one of Yonder's elderflower beers is available while the actual flowers are still out. That's not to say an elderflower beer can't be beautiful in winter – if anything it might be a welcome reminder of sunny, warmer times – but this one has exactly the right aroma at the right time of year. Usually any flavour in NEIPA that can't also be found in a carton of breakfast juice is considered an off flavour, but in this beer elderflower adds a freshness so often lacking in these big, juicy beers. DEYA's house IPA culture also gives the elderflower room to shine and even has a hint of florality to it – something you get in the brewery's seminal Steady Rolling Man.

For me, this beer is a wonderful example of how we can bring seasonality back into modern beer. We don't need to scrap our steel and boycott American hops, but we can make the most of what is around us by using it to fill in the flavour gaps left by ultra-modern processes and trends. What's more, the use of foraged and seasonal ingredients in such modern beer might help beer geeks re-establish that connection between the beer we drink and the world around us. We don't all have the privilege to know what the Yakima Valley smells like come September, but we certainly can understand what spring smells like when elderflower is in season – whether we're out in the wilds, or round the back of a sixties' leisure centre.

Revelling in the new warmth of summer

June

June feels like the most British month of the year. There is something very plastic-Union-Jack-waving about it that comes from a combination of Coronation day (2nd June), the Queen's 'official birthday' (second Saturday of June) and the start of Wimbledon (the rainiest week of June).

Such events inspire us ever-plucky Brits to pretend the fruit added to Pimm's is part of our five-a-day, talk endlessly about the weather, and indulge in other British-isms that make the rest of the world roll their eyes. Beer provides one of those things in the form of Beer Day Britain. Started by beer writer Jane Peyton, it's an annual celebration of our brewing heritage. We've bought into the warm and flat cliché so much that beer geeks often forget how our beer scene is revered by many other nations, and indeed was the inspiration behind the American brewing movement. So, not only is this a great month to have a few pints of classic cask, it's also a good time to see how far our scene has come. Whatever kind of beer you're into, whether it's tropical IPAs, Trappist beer, Norwegian farmhouse-style ale or Czech Lager, use this moment as an excuse to remember how well British brewers do it.

Another great British tradition is packing the beaches at the first sign of sun, where we wash down sandy sandwiches and drippy ice cream with bad beer. Our seaside towns were left almost to crumble when cheap pan-European flights became a reality, but some are having a renaissance and becoming wonderful places to visit whatever the weather. That's especially true of those that have adapted to serve great food and drink – places like Margate and Whitstable, Padstow and Falmouth, the coast of Northumberland, and of course Suffolk, home to the world-famous fish and chips of Aldeburgh.

What to drink

An emerging trend in the beer world is to have a sideline in gin distillation, either through distilling excess beer or simply teaming up with a distillery and using beer as inspiration. The classic British G&T is an early summer staple and there are lots of hybrids for the beer-focused drinker. Yonder Brewing have done a fantastic foraged Wild Flower gin, Tiny Rebel did a delicious spirit version of their Clwb Tropicana fruited Pale Ale, Harvey's have their own Eau De Vie that's just like Grappa (and is being aged to become whisky), and Wild Beer Co have also released several gins inspired by the fruits and spices of their mixed fermentation beers.

If you're sticking to beer, it's going to be what suits the outdoors – some of the seasonal wild beers we talked about in May, tides of delicious crispy Lagers, and the last of the spring IPAs will all make great outdoor beers and barbecue accompaniments.

What to eat

The most famous seasonal produce in June is, of course, the strawberry, but the actual season for these beautiful fruits is pretty broad, depending on variety, latitude and process. By June, though, there should be lots of beautiful, ripe British strawberries to pick. Try with a Flemish Red (like Wild Beer's Modus Operandi), which acts like the balsamic glaze that surprisingly brings out sweetness. We're also into broad bean season, one of my favourite vegetables and beautiful in spring chicken stews and salads with crumbly cheese – crying out for a Berliner Weisse or German Pilsner. If you're headed to the coast you already know what to eat: fish and chips followed by a 99!

What to do

Beer festival season is upon us and the UK is blooming with wonderful places to go. Fyne Ales up in Argyll is a beautifully isolated location for a festival, so (if you can cope with the midges) Fyne Fest is a highlight of the early beer calendar. You can also head to Bigfoot, a music festival run by the same people behind London Craft Beer Festival, which finally brings good beer to a weekend music event. You'll also find myriad local beer festivals all over the UK throughout the summer, with Liverpool, Nottingham and Cheltenham getting the party started. Increasingly, you can also get good beer while on holiday in the coastal towns of the UK, so if you're headed there make sure you support the independents.

Delicious crispy Lagers, and the last of the spring IPAs, will all make **great outdoor beers** and barbecue accompaniments

Micropubs

The future of Britain's high streets

'Water, water everywhere, nor any drop to drink' is a phrase I often used to think about while visiting the coastal resorts of the UK.

Things aren't quite as dire as they were for the Ancient Mariner, but good beer and tourist spots have never really mixed. Only big breweries and pub chains can afford such prime real estate, and even today those companies rarely offer the variety they should. That means whichever seaside town you visit you'll likely be confronted with the same mass-market Lagers and Bitters. I can't think of a worse beer and food match than a skunky Heineken and a 99 Flake, but at these high-rent, high-turnover locations the margin is king – not quality.

Over the last decade, however, around 500 businesses have found a workaround. The tragic decline of the high street has left thousands of British towns hollowed out in the middle, including those that should be buzzing in summer. As they say, though, when one door closes another opens ... and sometimes that door leads to a pub. The micropub is a brilliant and utterly British invention that gets around sky-high pub rents and ties by opening a fully licensed bar in a vacant shop. Not only are rental values significantly lower, but these shops are often on high footfall streets, with lots of natural light from the store fronts.

That's not to say there aren't challenges. You have to persuade the council to change the allowed usage of the property, and with no cellar you have to build a cold room into the footprint of the main floor. For this reason, many micropubs rely on bag-in-box beer rather than cask, and very few have any food offering to speak of. Even that has its charms, though. Good cider is often packaged in bag-in-box, which has resulted in micropubs often being the most reliable places to find tasty cider in the UK. The beer is also more likely to be bang-fresh, because each box can only hold up to 20 litres. On top of that, the lack of a kitchen means cheeky cheeseboards, meat platters and pickled eggs are the order of the day.

The micropub movement started in 2005 in Herne Bay, Kent, when Martyn Hillier converted his off-license – itself previously a butchers shop – into a mini pub. He called it The Butcher's Arms and did pretty much all the work himself to keep costs down. His aim was to offer somewhere simple and welcoming that was focused

The micropub is a **brilliant and utterly British** invention that gets around sky-high pub rents and ties by opening a fully-licensed bar in a vacant shop

on serving great cask beer, as well as to show that opening a pub is possible on a shoestring budget. The Butcher's Arms was a huge success, and led to him founding the Micropub Association shortly afterwards to help others achieve the same. As a result, the idea has spread all over the country, but Kent is still home to the highest concentration of them – in particular Thanet in its north-eastern corner.

Planet Thanet

Margate is a town in the midst of real change. When the annual stream of summer tourists slowed to a trickle in the 1980s it struggled for both identity and money. It was in decline for decades, but in the last 10 years or so the low rents started to attract a new kind of resident – the artists and tradespeople priced out of the

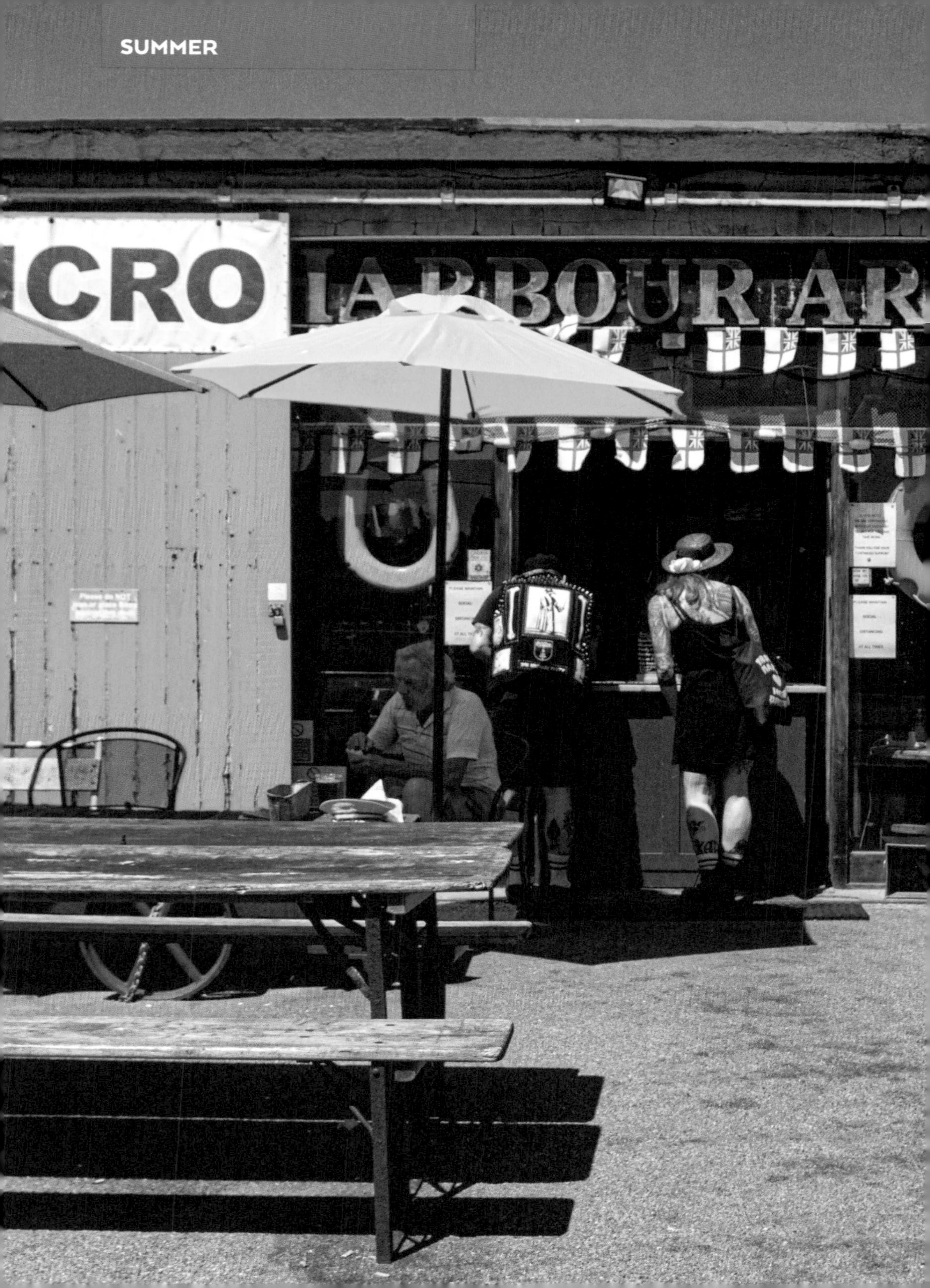
ICRO

creative hub of East London. The rise of this kind of industry has resulted in Margate being labeled Shoreditch-on-Sea, but it still retains so much of its original culture. Right now it's a wonderful mix of retro British charm and a modern, artisanal outlook – a combination embodied by the micropub revolution.

Found on the pier looking back across the harbour to the seafront, there's no argument that the Harbour Arms has the best location. Housed in two old fishermen's sheds, it still has huge orange doors on wheels, and bric-a-brac from a time when the harbour would have been filled with boats rather than sunburned swimmers. There aren't many seats, but that's OK because you can buy pints to take away and wander up the stone stairs to the roof, where you can look straight out to sea with nothing between you and (depending which way you turn) Essex, the Netherlands or Norway. If you do grab a seat there's some wonderful people-watching to be had. Tourists will head past you to get a close look at the Margate Lighthouse (the one you'll find on a £20 note) and in summer there are occasional live music nights, too. On tap you'll find three real ales and a wider selection of ciders, but whatever you choose you're not going to pay more than £4, which leaves plenty of change to invest in their wide array of pickled eggs and onions.

I'm not sure there are many places in the world where you can grab **a few IPAs, farmhouse cheeses, pâté and crackers** then walk a few metres onto the sand, but every resort should have something similar

Just about visible from the Harbour Arms is a very different kind of micropub. Little Swift has been many things in its life, including a telecommunications shop and a seafood restaurant, but now it's the most incredible little bar and deli right across from the beach. It's run by Charlotte Kimber and Steve Taylor, who used to run the pub for beer distributor The Bottle Shop. When that company went under the pair scraped together enough money to reopen it on their own terms. It was a nice place to drink beforehand, but now it's one of the best little pubs in the country.

You can sit in and admire the view right across the bay while eating artisan meat boards and drinking through the six taps of draught beer, massive wine collection and two tall beer fridges. The beer comes from all over the world, but there's always room for local brewing heroes Gadd's – at a crisp 1.2% ABV, the brewery's No11 Pale Ale is the perfect afternoon beer.

During the 2020 lockdown half the pub was converted into a shop, so you can also buy some bits to-go and cross the road to the beach. I'm not sure that there are many places in the world where you can grab a few IPAs, farmhouse cheeses, pâté and crackers then walk a few metres straight onto the sand, but every resort should have something similar.

Just a few doors down is the Two Halves, a multi-CAMRA-award-winning micropub that can fully open its front onto the sea, but equally good beer can be found if you double back on yourself up the High Street and walk on to Fez. Owned by the enigmatic Phil Evans, you'd never know Fez used to be a shop. Phil has ripped up the old grey carpet to reveal multi-coloured tiles that inspired the remarkable decor. Almost every inch of the walls and floor is covered with retro finds from flea markets around the UK. You can sit in an early 20th century barber's chair or a classic Waltzer dual bonquet, or even settle into some 1930s' German cinema seats, which Phil says he bought in Rotherham of all places. Above you hang hundreds of trinkets from bygone eras, mostly from the UK brewing, car and tobacco industries, peppered with references to other countries such as Mexico and Morocco.

The beer list is small but perfectly formed and beautifully kept. On my last visit, the head on my Kent Golding Bitter summited nearly an inch above the rim and lasted the whole way down the pint. It was loaded with Hovis biscuit sweetness and the berry notes of Kent's famous Golding hops – a quintessential British Bitter. On top of the excellent cask you'll find some delicious bag-in-box ciders and over 30 different gins – another passion of Phil's. If you get hungry there are Tunnocks Wafers and Teacakes on the bar. I can't promise they'll go with what you're drinking, but I'm also certain you won't care.

It's not really the beer or the wafers that makes Fez such a wonderful place to drink, however. Phil is often sat at the main table, welcoming everyone who comes through the door – and nine times out of ten he knows them. In fact, I was the only stranger in the bar the last time I went in, and I still received a local's welcome.

Micropubs are intimate by their nature, but they seem specifically designed to feel like an old friend's living room. The low costs of setting one up means you get the dreamers and the borderline hobbyists indulging their passion projects and putting their heart and soul into them. That gives all these pubs an individual character that breathes life back into our struggling high streets, and feels a million miles away from the chain pubs just around the corner.

You can still see the scars of Margate's decline through the 1980s but now they're the backdrop to the town's newfound joy and vitality. To anyone who says 'it's just beer', I like to point out how micropubs, their owners and their customers, have played their part in turning the town of Margate around.

Micropubs are **intimate by their nature,** but they seem specifically designed to feel like **an old friend's living room**

The seafood diet

Making the most of our coastal cuisine

Not all seafood has to come out of the sea. Some of it is made in the tacky looking shop; the ice cream van that's seen better days; the trailer that hasn't moved in a decade.

I could write a book solely about the food that springs up around our beaches, and how it echoes our culture nearly as loudly as our beer. We are blessed by being an island nation, with so much coastline and so much variation, but the food we enjoy there is roughly the same wherever you land. We all know about the cockles, ice cream and fish and chips, but there are some more curious cuisines associated with the sea. Rock is one of those things I file next to quicksand and toys in cereal packets as things that only mattered when we were kids, and yet it's still everywhere. Doughnuts are also an unlikely seafood snack, and yet most seaside towns will have at least one place serving them up, usually to some very over-excited teens.

Until recently we didn't have much choice about what we drank down at the coast, but the micropub revolution and the rise of the independent bottle shop means there's pretty much good beer to be had everywhere. Rather than grimacing our way through a warm can of Kronenberg 1664 with our fish and chips, there's a chance of finding a combination worthy of the setting. So next time you're headed to the seaside, look up the local bottle shops, breweries and micropubs and grab something tasty to put in the cooler ready for those spontaneous foodie purchases. Perhaps for the first time ever in print, this is the ultimate guide to matching British seafront food with good beer.

Fish and chips

Like so much of our cuisine, battered fish was brought to the UK by immigrants. In this case it was Jewish settlers in the 17th century, who would have fried fish in flour to create a crust. Since then, we've embellished it with liquid to create a crispy batter that we've bathed in as a nation for centuries since.

Fish and chips are so much a part of our DNA that George Orwell wrote about how it helped sate the workers and prevented revolution. Perhaps suspecting the same, it was one of the few meals not touched by the government when introducing rationing for the Second World War – although the price did rise steeply. Recently we've combined this British institution with our brewing heritage by making the batter with beer, further solidifying fish and chips' claim to be our national dish. While the choice of beer in the batter doesn't matter too much, the choice of drink with it matters a whole lot. Any beer we put with deep-fried fish should have either acidity or hop bitterness to cut through the copious amounts of oil and potato. A Gose is a brilliant idea, bringing some extra salinity to the seafood party while topping up the malt vinegar tang. The classic match is, of course, a British Bitter, but if you're going for one of those it's probably better in bottle because it will have sharper bubbles, and the paler and hoppier the better. Timothy Taylor's Landlord and Adnams Ghost Ship are both perfection.

The 99 Flake

The 99 Flake may cost two or even three times the 99p it did originally, but I still defy anyone to tell me it isn't worth every penny. The texture is second to none, as is that glorious mix of creamy milk and sweet vanilla. Sure, the flake tastes of next to nothing when your palate is frozen, and the cone feels like it's 80% recycled cardboard, but somehow the combination is addictive. The need for a 99 while down at the seafront is almost Pavlovian.

As we have already explored in this book, contrasting temperatures are a challenge for our palates to deal with, and very sweet food is tricky to match with beer. So my first bit of advice is to eat the flake first, while your palate can still detect its flavour. Use it as a spoon, revel in its practical but delicious form. Once done, you'll have a spare hand for the beer, which needs to be the sweetest thing you can find. Imperial and Pastry Stouts will be the best – and often have vanilla in them already. A coffee-infused one might even create a trashy Affogato vibe.

You could also go for a clean, fruited kettle sour. Brett would be distracting here, but lactobacillus (which is used to make yoghurt) is the perfect souring bacteria to go with sweetness and the fruit is like adding compote. If you've shelled out for a fancy 99 – perhaps with chocolate and nuts and a waffle cone – a Maibock would be seasonal and delicious, as if you'd drizzled caramel on top.

Fresh or pickled cockles

For some reason I am always surprised to see somewhere selling cockles. It feels like food from a bygone era, but every time I taste some I remember why they endure. They are sweet, salty and textured like the best plump mussel, and usually saturated in vinegar like a perfect soggy chip. For these I'd advise the same approach we took for oysters in March. You need minerality, roasty savouriness and body: and that means a Stout. A good Irish Dry Stout or Porter will soften the acidity and bring out sweetness, and even taste good should the sun make it a little warmer that you wanted it.

A doorstep crab sandwich

Crab is one of the most underrated foods in the UK. What it lacks in the texture of lobster or langoustine it more than makes up for in salty, umami and fresh flavours. The white meat also has an unmistakable butteriness that makes it the ultimate sandwich filler at the seaside. All it needs is a dash of lemon, some greens for a crunch and potentially mayonnaise to pad it out. A seeded brown loaf is the ultimate vessel for delivery, and it should float on something zesty and refreshing like a straight-up Berliner Weisse. You could also go for a Witbier, which will have more body and sweetness to echo the sandwich rather than contrast it, or a really bright and zesty cask Golden or Pale Ale that will complement the brown bread but cut through the mayo. Verdant Lightbulb is the perfect accompaniment if you're in Cornwall, the home of great British crab.

Dressed-up lobster

In June we're right at the start of native lobster season, and despite the eye-watering price, local pot-caught lobster is relatively sustainable and absolutely delicious. The meat is sweet, fleshy and very lightly salted compared to crab, which means it needs a much more delicate touch when it comes to what you drink with it. Champagne is the classic match, and not only because it too is absurdly decadent: more importantly it's crisp, fruity and highly carbonated to cut through. A really clean and dry Saison, Belgian Strong (similar to Duvel) or Tripel can achieve the same thing, although some of these beers can have a little too much estery character, so go for the lighter ABVs within those style guidelines. One of the UK's great seaside experiences can be found at the Lobster Shack in Whitstable, with a plastic pint of crisp Pale Ale and a plate of lobster and chips.

Handfuls of calamari and whitebait

White bait and calamari instantly transport me to the Mediterranean, where I'd be ordering a crisp Sauvignon Blanc rather than the local, likely boring, mass-made Lager. In the UK we have a bit more choice, and these crispy, oily and fishy snacks

are great with almost any beer with a cracker-dry malt body and ideally a little hop character to emphasise the lemon you should liberally squeeze all over the fish. German and Italian Pilsners, Helles, Berliner Weisses and mixed fermentation Saisons are all ideal. The absolute best beer would be Burning Sky's Petit Saison, with its crisp and light body, gentle sourness and lemony finish.

A big Cornish pasty

There are three places where you can get Cornish pasties: Cornwall, the seaside, and Gatwick Airport train station. To be honest, I would only really recommend the first one.

The story is that pasties were originally meals for miners, who would eat the stuffed middle section and dispose of the thick, crimped crust which they had been holding with their dirty hands. But photos show most were eaten from paper or muslin, which suggests it's more likely the miners just really liked pastry. It also maintains structure so the pastry is easier to eat, especially when you have a beer in your hand, which you definitely should. I have many happy memories of drinking St Austell Tribute while demolishing a beef pasty after a long, rainy and windy Cornish hike. For that reason I can't think of a better match. Go for something with lots of malt character, whether it's biscuit and sweet or roasty and coffee-like. If you go for a cheese and onion one, keep the malt notes, but find something really hoppy too, because mature Cheddar and bitter hops really help one another sing. Staying with St Austell, Proper Job is the ideal beer.

Freshly fried donuts

I guess with a lot of fryers on the coast it was inevitable something sweet would go in there eventually, and there's nothing like a still-warm donut dipped deep into sugar and (ideally) cinnamon, too. The sight of kids running gleefully back to the beach clutching bags so oily they've gone see-through is synonymous with summer holidays for me.

These oily, decadent balls of batter are brilliant for beer matching, being full of simple flavours and missing the one thing that donuts are famous for: jam. So it's clear that they need one thing: a fruit sour. Which flavour is entirely up to you, though the thicker and sillier the better. Try a North Brewing Co Triple Fruited Sour, or one of Kernel's more nuanced Bière de Saisons (the Damson one would be utterly amazing). Another perfect match would be a Dark Mild, where the sweet caramel and milk chocolate vibes would have a very different but equally delicious effect on the donut. You can turn that up to 11 by choosing an Imperial Stout, especially good if the weather has let you down and that dip in the sea means you're now in need of something warming.

These oily, decadent **balls of batter** are **brilliant for beer matching,** being full of simple flavour

SHELLFISH

DRESSED CRABS
(AS PRICED)

LOBSTER WHOLE

LOBSTER ½ DRESSED

POTTED SHRIMP £5

PEELED PRAWNS
SML £2·50
LRG £5

COCKLES
SML £2·50
LRG £5

SHELL ON PRAWNS
£5 a PINT

NEW Potted Lobster
£5

OPEN
Please come in we are

WE ONLY
TAKE
CASH
NOT
CARDS
SORRY

PRICE LIST

COD WHOLE
COD FILLETS
SEABASS WHOLE
SEABASS FILLETS
DOVER SOLES SM
MED
LRG
SKATE WINGS
ROCK EEL

WE ONLY
TAKE
CASH
NOT CARDS
SORRY

HAND GEL

Beer-battered fish

Our national dish done right

It's not really a pub meal or trip to the seaside if someone doesn't order beer-battered fish. I can't think of a better way to spend a sunny June day than in a pub garden or on a harbour wall with a plate of fish and chips and a hoppy Golden Ale.

Unfortunately though, the quality varies nearly as wildly as the price. Like all simple things in life, getting the batter right is devilishly tricky. I've made a lot of beer-battered fish in my time but I've only recently discovered that the secret is not the temperature of the oil (although that is vital) but the carbonation and temperature of the batter.

For years I was struggling to get that crispy and flaky texture, upping my oil temp and thinning out the batter to the point when I was basically just setting fire to flour. But then I found a recipe by the amazing food writer Felicity Cloake that changed all that. The important thing is the contrast in temperature at the moment the fish goes in the fryer – that's what makes the batter almost explode, as the carbonation races out and makes millions of tiny nucleation sites for the oil to latch onto and turn crispy. For that to happen, the batter needs to be freezing. The key is to put both the beer and the flour in the fridge hours before cooking, and to make mix it seconds before you start cooking.

When it comes to the beer, however, you don't need to be anywhere near as prescriptive. I've tried several different styles and even really strong bitterness can't stand the heat flavour-wise. The important thing is the carbonation, which helps the batter puff up when it hits the oil. That said, just using fizzy water does seem to remove a little flavour, so the best bet is to use a decent, well-carbonated Golden Ale or Pilsner to ensure some maillard reaction and tease out a little depth.

INGREDIENTS

Dripping or oil, for frying (deep enough for your size of fish)

380g plain flour, straight from the fridge

3tsp baking powder

500ml very cold beer, straight from the fridge

4 pieces of sustainable white fish (pollock or haddock, probably)

METHOD

1 Heat the oil to 185°C – if you don't have a thermometer go buy one, you don't want to estimate this. Meanwhile, get some kitchen paper and lay it out on a plate ready for the cooked fish.

2 Once you're absolutely ready to cook, get the flour out the fridge and quickly mix with the baking powder and a good pinch of granular salt. Even more quickly, whisk in the ice cold beer until smooth, then dip the fish in so it's coated.

3 Carefully place in the fryer and agitate the oil gently, which stops it sticking and gives the batter a rough texture. Don't cook more than two fillets at a time or else you'll drop the temperature of the oil too far. Cook for about 5 mins, maybe a shade more if it's a big fillet, then place on the kitchen paper to drip dry for 1 min.

4 Plate up with chips, mushy peas and more salt and vinegar than looks sensible, then serve with an ice-cold Gose or English Pale Ale.

July

The British summer is roughly ten days long, broken up by much longer periods of humid, breezy and pretty drizzly weeks. So when the sun does come out, we're famous worldwide for making the most of it. That usually translates into red faces, t-shirt suntans, mile-long lines at the ice cream van, and pint after pint of Lager.

These beers were first brewed in the hotter climes of central Europe, where Lager yeasts were the dominant natural fermenting microbe. There's been lots of academic research into why such yeasts, which prefer to ferment cold, should be so ascendant in a region with fiercely hot summers. The most compelling argument I've heard is that it was natural selection: a hybridisation caused by German brewers keeping their ferments cold in rocky cellars and caves, and repeatedly cropping yeast from the bottom. This resulted in super-clean fermentations, and influenced what the brewers made – namely, increasingly light, pale and malty beers that suited the weather.

Let's be honest, though, there aren't many people puzzling through this particular quirk of history. Come July,

sensible people are too busy drinking them. In this chapter we'll look at why it took the UK so long to get excited about Lager, and how it went too far in its pursuit of crispiness. Our eventual obsession with Pale Lager means there's a lot of bad Lager out there, but increasingly there are some great ones too. Many beer lovers have dismissed them as dull and bland, but understanding their true nature and how much they vary is key to finding one you really enjoy. Context is also important, too. A Pilsner by the fire in winter won't have anywhere near the quenching effect of one in a sunny beer garden.

What to drink

When we talk about Lager we probably all picture the same thing – a honey-coloured, highly carbonated pint that smells softly of digestive biscuits and lemon. But it's worth remembering that Lager is a family of styles, not a style itself. So while a crisp, hoppy Pilsner or a sweeter Helles might be perfect in summer – so might a lovely Bock, or an India Pale Lager, or even a Baltic Porter once the sun's down. They all taste very different, but they still finish with the signature snap that Lager yeasts create and makes them so darn moreish. I implore you to ignore the Untappd ratings or rants of hopheads and real ale snobs when it comes to these beautiful styles. Be curious, be open minded and give them all a go – especially if they come from Donzoko, Lost and Grounded, Braybrooke or Utopian.

What to eat

There's never a safe time of year to plan a British barbecue but July seems the most sensible option – even if it does rain you'll still be warm. All you need is stubbornness and an umbrella you trust not to burst into flames at the mere sight of hot coals. To be controversial, though, burgers and sausages aren't at their best over a barbecue. It takes a pro to control the heat well enough to caramelise the outside and keep the inside moist. Much easier are quick-cooking meats – marinated skewered chicken and veg, Indian-spiced lamb chops and hanger steaks, or ribbons of courgette, asparagus and tenderstem broccoli coated in salt, pepper, olive oil and lemon juice.

Where to go

Despite the long conditioning time, great Lager is best drunk fresh, just like IPA. That's why I visit breweries more in summer than in winter: Pilsner and Helles taste best direct from the source, and breweries are notoriously cold and drafty places in winter anyway. In this chapter I'll give you my favourite al fresco drinking locations, and thankfully most good breweries will have a decent Pilsner on tap these days, so you can combine a love of fresh hops and Lager into one visit. If you're looking for beery event, Bristol Craft Beer Festival is a great weekend in the glorious sunshine of Bristol harbour, with lots of fringe nights, too.

Great Lager is **best drunk fresh,** just like IPA. That's why I visit breweries more in summer than in winter: **Pilsner and Helles taste best direct from the source**

About time

The start of Britain's Lager revolution

Despite having an ideal climate for cold fermentation and storage, the UK was slow on the uptake with Pale Lager. Pilsners had come to dominate mainland Europe by the early 20th century, but on this side of the channel we clung on to our traditional beers like drinkers at closing time. In fact, ale outsold Lager right up until the late eighties.

The reasons are myriad and complicated, but I should start by pointing out that without British brewing expertise, the rise of modern Lager might have happened a lot later than it did. Pale Lager was supposedly invented in 1842 by Josef Groll of the newly founded Pilsner Urquell. It's fair to say he invented what we now call the Bohemian Pilsner, but actually the Lagers from neighbouring Germany and Austria had been pretty pale for a few years by then. The true origin of Pale Lager seems to lie in a tour of English and Scottish breweries by Spaten's Gabriel Sedlmayr and Anton Dreher, who went on to found Vienna's Schwechater Brewery.

During that research trip they learned about the UK's advanced malting techniques, which made paler, less smoky malt possible. On their return, they combined those malts with Sedlmayr's Lager yeast to make the first Märzens around 1839. The commercial success of those beers, as well as Groll's Pilsner three years later, meant beers all over continental Europe started turning pale or being replaced by lighter versions – a trend accelerated in the late 1800s with Von Linde's refrigeration breakthrough and the isolation (and then spread) of a specific Lager yeast by Emil Hansen at Carlsberg in 1883.

In the UK at that time, though, Dark Mild was in the ascendency and would remain the most popular beer style until after the Second World War. It wasn't that British drinkers didn't come across these continental Lagers. In fact, Sedlmayr had made friends with John Muir of Edinburgh's Muir & Sons brewery during his tour of the UK in the 1830s, and sent him some Lager yeast on his return home. Muir brewed a Pale Lager that I imagine amazed local drinkers with its clarity and clean finish, but issues in propagating the yeast meant the experiment was short-lived.

Lager also had a brief spell of trendiness in the UK in the late 1860s, when the great and the good tried the Pale Lagers of Vienna at the Great Exhibition in Paris. This was followed by an extraordinarily hot summer that drove enough demand for

What started as the **premium option** had crashed right through the mainstream to **monopolise the industry**

five London venues to start stocking imported Märzen. Unfortunately, being triple the price of a pint of Mild meant few could afford such an extravagance, so while there was German-style Pale Lager available in the UK from then on, it was never more than an interesting niche for those rich enough to try it. I enjoy the image of outraged Brits asking 'HOW much for a pint?!' even 150 years ago.

The reason it wasn't really brewed in the UK for nearly a century is a little harder to pin down, but I think the UK's malts, and, particularly hops, weren't ideal for the style. All our breweries were also well set up for top cropping, and not for long chilling. Up until after the Second World War there's also British exceptionalism, anti-German sentiment and the dominance of the regional ale brewers to think about, too. Some writers have mused about the idea that the UK climate didn't create such a need for Pilsner, but there were much colder parts of the world (namely Denmark) that had embraced Lager wholeheartedly. It's also a theory blown out of the water by just how absurdly popular it became when the dam finally broke and a tide of continental Lagers washed over the UK. In 1965 it was just 2% of the market, but by 1989 it was over 50%, buoyed by its consistency and the idyllic image of Europe left by summer holidays – an image exploited by leading brands like Stella Artois.

By 2008 Pale Lager represented 75% of the UK beer market. What started as the premium option had crashed right through the mainstream to monopolise the industry. But along the way, many breweries in the UK and Europe had lost sight of what made the original beer style so brilliant. Local hops were forsaken and replaced with higher alpha foreign varieties, floor malts were replaced by mass-germinated grains, open fermenters scrapped, and chemicals used to speed up the manufacturing process. Soon there was little to connect the original long-matured Lagers of Bavaria and Bohemia to the palid, dull Pilsners that were now fermented and packaged in a matter of days.

So it's understandable that the world's various craft beer revolutions left Lager brewing to the big guns. If anything, craft beer was a reaction against the hegemonic world of Pale Lager. New British beer lovers wanted rich malt flavours and bold hop finishes, neither of which were provided by what we knew as Lager back then. It was thin, over-carbonated and everywhere; a race to the bottom in pricing and flavour.

Of course, that's not really what Lager is and I remember my first pint of proper Pilsner as vividly as I do my first IPA. It was a Pilsner Urquell in East London served unpasteurised from a tank, via a side-pour tap into a handled jug. It smelled like dulce de leche on warm crusty bread, with notes of lemon and something strawberry-like too if you really inhaled it. It was velvet on my tongue, moreish as salty crisps and fresh as a sprinkled lawn. On the finish it was bitter and prickly, the thorn on a rose. That first pint didn't last five minutes, and I was left wondering why such beers weren't made in the UK.

A few early UK craft breweries did try to bring great Lager to discerning drinkers: Meantime Brewing Company's founder, Alistair Hook, was trained at Weihenstephaner in Bavaria; Freedom Lager has been producing pretty good Pilsners since 2007; while Camden Town Brewery pushed its excellent Hells hardest of all its beers. But they have all learned that making and selling lots of Lager in the UK is a numbers game, because it's seen as a cheap commodity. Both Meantime and Camden sold to international conglomerates to make the financials work, and Freedom has never quite realised its promise. Meanwhile, it took hop-loving breweries a long time to come around to the idea of tying up their tanks for weeks, only to compete on price with some of the world's biggest companies. Thankfully, as the collective UK palate matured, demand for proper Lager has increased and the UK now has a burgeoning, varied Lager brewing scene.

We all know that Pale Lager is the ultimate summer drink: the image of an ice cold, condensation-coated bottle that slakes your thirst without touching the sides is the basis upon which Lager's empire was built. But what this message tends to lose is the diversity within Lager brewing. Most beer geeks still think of Lager as a boring necessity come summer, and to them I say there is a fine but very important line between boring and subtle. We now have breweries focusing on endless different Lager styles – not just Pilsner and Helles, but lesser known ones like Bocks, Italian Pilsners, Franconian Kellerbiers, Bohemian Dark Lagers and Baltic Porters. On top of that there has been a burst of unique recipes and approaches that mean, for the first time in our country's long history, we have a diverse and exciting selection of beers to choose from when the weather really warms and the world opens up. Being aware of that opens up as many opportunities as a sunny weekend.

Just like ale, Lager isn't a style – it's a family of beers, defined by the use of yeasts that like to mature at much lower temperatures than ale ones. Within that family are distinguishable styles that are perfect for different occasions and tastes. We've already covered a few of them earlier in the book, so here I'm going to focus on the pale, pintable ones we reach for when the mercury rises. While it may be tempting to drink these beers by the litre Maß (it's a Maß, not a Stein – Steins are made of stone), you're better off with smaller glasses so you don't end up with warm dregs.

German Pilsner

Let's start with the German Pilsner. This style bears closest resemblance to the macro-Lagers that still make up around 70% of what British people drink. It's cracker dry, with light hay and honey notes, and a subtle hoppiness that packs a little bite alongside the Lager yeast. It's the ultimate quenching beer, designed to be drunk in ungodly quantities and ideally used to wash down pretzels and sausages. Most craft Lagers in the UK are based on these beers because of their mass market appeal. Pressure Drop are an example of a hop-led brewery that makes fantastic Pilsners (often in January when they have had Christmas to mature), and Left Handed Giant do great draught Pilsners at their two breweries, and sometimes in can, too.

If German Pilsner sounds a little plain, there's still a lot of variation to be found, usually through the use of exciting hops. Modern German varieties like Hallertau Blanc (think white wine acidity) and Petit Blanc (berries and acacia) have added depth to Donzoko Brewing's Pilsners, while New Zealand Motueka is used in lots of Pils because it's a descendant of the classic Czech Lager hop, Saaz. It has the same soft and round bitterness, but also adds lemon and lime notes that make Braybrooke's NZ Pils even more suitable for summer. These modern interpretations are often hopped much later to keep the light nature of the beers intact, but offer up

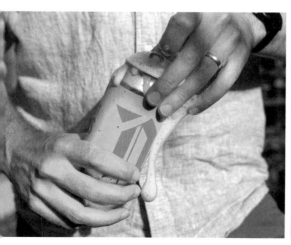

lots of enticing aroma. Cloudwater Brew Co regularly put out incredibly bright Pilsners, mixing up the hopping schedule between UK and German varieties to keep their hop-loving customers coming back for more.

Helles

German's other great Lager style is the Helles, which was (predictably) invented by Spaten Brauerei as a session-strength alternative to its Märzen. This light, golden beer has lots of honey and even brioche malt tones to it, usually with a less dry and hoppy finish than a Pilsner. That means it can feel like it has a bit more body and richness, but should retain the drinkability of a Pilsner over a session. Examples of this style used to be pretty rare in the UK, partly because brewers didn't trust drinkers to know what a Helles is, and partly because it's not quite as immediate as a Pilsner.

The rise of interest in small-batch Lager has driven a renaissance of these more malt-driven Lagers, however. Donzoko's Northern Helles combines that sticky, bready malt bill with a dose of its own tangy lactic culture (to ensure crispiness and complexity) and a sprinkle of New Zealand hops that add a floral quality to the beer. Bristol's Lost and Grounded make a stellar, slightly drier example and even package it in Bavarian-style 500ml bottles. Thornbridge's Lukas is, perhaps, the best in the UK and might even be the best beer in a portfolio that includes the peerless Jaipur. Lukas's aroma is rich, floral and deep, but it's somehow brighter and more refreshing than any other Helles I've had. And I include any from Munich in that.

Kellerbier

While we're talking about Munich Lagers, it's worth taking a little detour to talk about Kellerbier. This word actually describes two very different kinds of Lager, so knowing which you're picking up is important. A Munich Kellerbier is an unfiltered, unpasteurised and therefore (hopefully) super-fresh version of Helles, and tastes as it would if consumed direct from the tank in the cellar. It's a little hazy and often tinged with Hefeweizen-like yeast aromas of banana and clove. Those soft fruit and spice notes mean it is not nearly as crisp as a Helles or Pilsner, but I think it's a brilliant spring and autumn alternative and still the kind of beer you can't stop sipping. Lost and Grounded's flagship Kellerpils is in this vein, being unpasteurised and only lagered for a couple of weeks to make it feel a little rustic and fresh, but they have brought back that lightning finish by upping the bitterness and making the beer really dry. If I had to pick any British Lager to drink for the rest of my summers, it would be this one.

If you drive a few hundred miles north of Munich to Franconia, however, the Kellerbier is something quite different. They should still be unfiltered and unpasteurised, but a Franconian Kellerbier is traditionally much darker – hovering somewhere around a Märzen or even darker. That adds raisin and toffee aromas, as well as lots of perceived sweetness. While I'd never try to imply a beer is healthy, there are few beers in the world that feel as nourishing and wholesome. There's also no beer garden culture quite like the one in Franconia, and the beers they drink there feel designed to be consumed in warm temperatures because they taste nearly as good at the warm end of the glass as they do at the cold start. Only one brewery makes this style really well in the UK so far, and that's Braybrooke. Drinking it 'vom Fass' – that's to say, from the barrel – overlooking the fields at the Braybrooke farm during harvest is one of those beer moments I'll never forget.

Czech Pilsner

And so we come to the style that started the worldwide revolution in Lager brewing, or at least the one credited with it: Czech Pilsner. While Spaten invented the pale Lager with their Märzen, the Helles was a response to the paler, low-strength Pilsners across the border. The Czech Republic has a rich and varied brewing culture, but most of the beers are based around their native pale malts, Lager yeasts and inimitable Saaz hops. There are over 400 breweries in a country of just 11 million people, and each one seems to make Lager with its own character, albeit stitched together by the almost pervasive use of one slightly outmoded technique: decoction.

Decoction is a little like the Lambic turbid mash. Most modern breweries use a 'single infusion' – meaning the grain and water are added at the same time and kept at a certain temperature. With decoction, a portion of the mash is drawn off and boiled, before being returned to the tun to raise the overall temperature. It was used back when grain wasn't as well processed and had to be taken up through various temperatures to get the best efficiency. Today our malt gives up its sugar extremely easily, but the caramelisation of the malts during that super-heating has a flavour impact, too. And the Czechs swear by it.

Together with the Saaz and local malts, it helps to create the heady mix of brioche, caramel and floral notes. Just how heady the aroma and flavour are

It's easy to understand why these kinds of **Lager** are **so enjoyable on warm days.** Being honey-sweet and only a little bitter, they **taste great** when served ice cold

depends on the strength of the beer. Utopian's Tenner is a 4% dry and snappy Lager with only hints of the saturated hop aroma of a Bohem's rich 4.9% Amos. Manchester Union's Lager is somewhere in between the two, and the closest any UK brewery has come to brewing a beer that rivals Pilsner Urquell. Served from a side pour tap – as all these beers should be – with that glorious, meringue-like foam is like being in Pilsen itself.

It feels a little wrong to mention Beak Brewery's Déšť as it's not decocted or purely hopped with Czech varieties, but there's no denying that it has that caramelised grain character and sweet hop aroma – all cut through with a hint of sulphur and grass that it borrows from German Pilsner and the Mittelfruh hops that go in with the Saaz. It's not traditional, but it's exceptionally tasty – and the can design is the embodiment of what these beers should look, taste and feel like to drink.

It's easy to understand why these kinds of Lager are so enjoyable on warm days. Being honey-sweet and only a little bitter, they taste great when served ice cold, unlike a lot of styles that lose their identity at low temperatures. They're also extremely easy drinking, and their more nuanced character means you can have quite a few before your palate gets tired. All of that is no coincidence – it's the reciprocal relationship of nature and human creation, of fermentation influencing brewers and brewers influencing fermentation.

Large-scale brewers of Lager have a lot to answer for in the breaking of that relationship. In a bid for efficiency and scale, they found ways of compressing fermentation and conditioning time into just days. This was mostly done by brewing in huge quantities, adding chemicals and fermenting at insane speeds and temperatures to a high alcohol level, then simply liquoring back to the required strength. In many cases the ABV is the only thing that sets these 'Lager' brands

apart. Drinkers came to expect the same flavours time after time, even if they switched brand or brewery. Through marketing the refreshing nature, golden colour and absolute clarity (rather than the provenance and variation), brewers convinced drinkers that this was what beer was meant to taste like – and had always tasted like. Really, it barely tasted of anything, but you knew what to expect and you knew if you were thirsty it would work.

If I could change one thing about British beer culture it would be to persuade people to appreciate a properly made Lager, and the wonderful nuance within it. I hope one day we'll have a Lager culture like that of Bavaria and Czechia, where every town has its own small-batch Lager brewery, celebrated for its individualism rather than its conformity. The craft beer revolution was an attempt to distance beer from macro Pale Lager, but wouldn't the ultimate victory be for small brewers to co-opt it? The ability to travel around the UK's beer gardens and taprooms drinking markedly different Lagers would truly be a victory for the seasons and for beer.

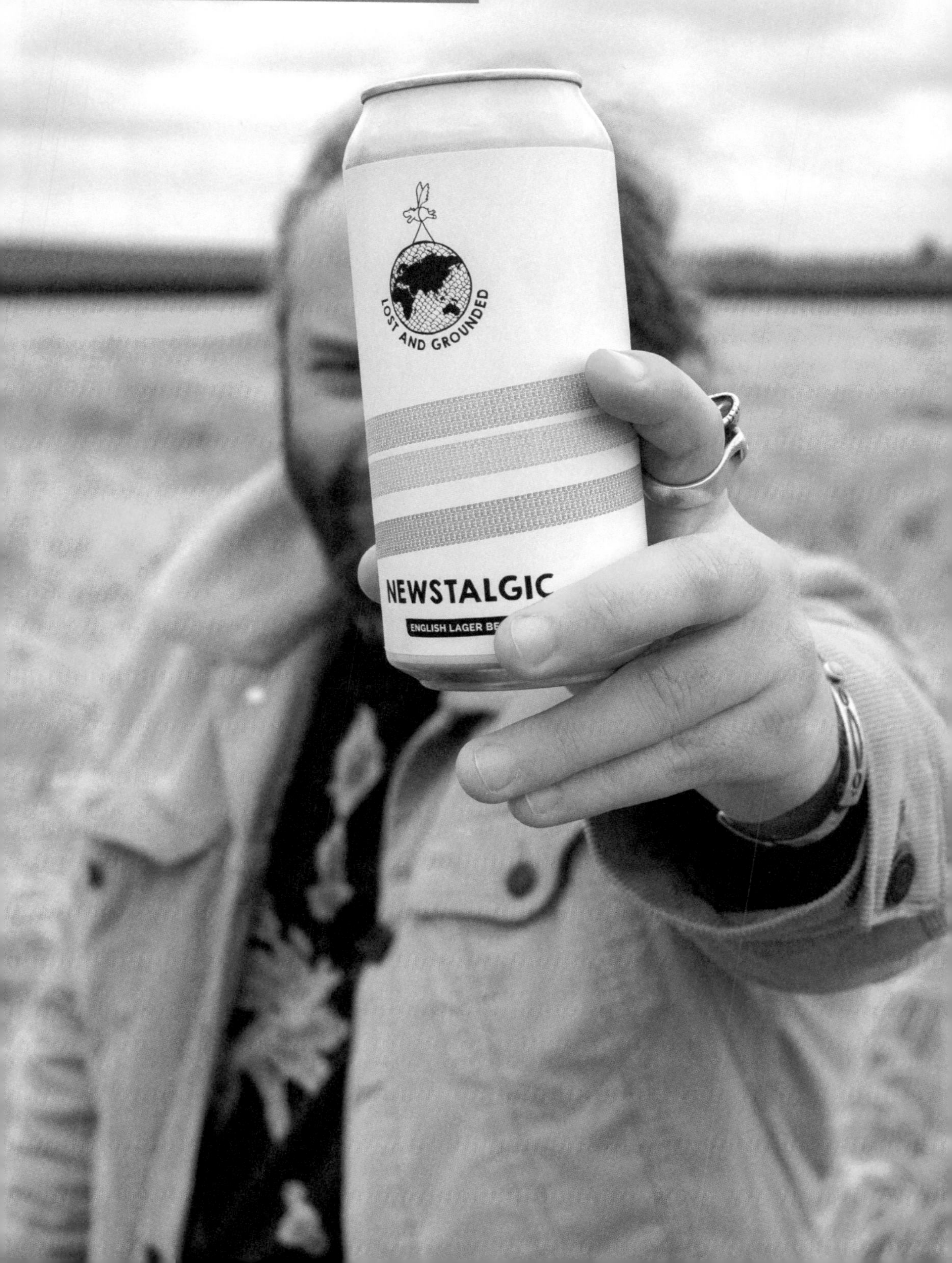
LOST AND GROUNDED
NEWSTALGIC
ENGLISH LAGER BE

Outdoor drinking

Getting back to nature

Drinking beer outside is one of the great pleasures in life, and it's not just the warm sun on your face and the cold beer in the glass. Well, actually it probably is just that (what more could you want?) but there's something else that stitches all that together.

The link between nature and beer has been almost entirely broken. We've not only lost the seasonal aspect, we've come detached the raw agricultural ingredients – the crunchy kilned malts, the sticky and resinous hops, the living, multiplying yeasts. Whether you're literally drinking next to a barley field, or simply taking in some rolling hills, I firmly believe that drinking outdoors can help reforge a connection that's lost through endless months spent inside hiding from the elements. I like to think that when we drink a beer outside we make a small, subconscious connection between the natural flavours and the natural environment. That's why beer just seems to taste better in the open.

There are, of course, all kinds of different outdoor experiences to be had in the UK beer scene – from Constable-like pastoralism to graffitied urbanity. Until recently, craft brewing had mostly happened in the towns and cities. That was where most of the pubs were, after all. But for drinkers wanting brewery fresh beer that meant industrial estates, drafty warehouses, and hard fold-out seating. Don't get me wrong, I love those places – beer is a manufacturing business as well as an agricultural one, and being around that is incredibly exciting. But as a comfortable space to bring family and friends less enamoured with beer, they leave a little to be desired. The last few years, however, have seen a burst of creativity from farms looking to diversify and pubs looking to attract younger clientele. There are now some breathtakingly beautiful countryside places to drink fantastic beer, some entirely isolated and some just a few minutes out of our major hubs. The only question is who drives.

So these are, in my experience, the best places to drink outside in the UK – carefully balancing the need for both world-class beer and a sense of being removed from the daily grind of the world. There are lots I've missed and will rue not having discovered before writing this book, but I've included both rural and urban destinations for diversity and access. Either way, these places will help us feel a little closer to our beer – whether through the nature, food, people or just being miles away from anything else.

Drinking outdoors can help **reforge a connection** that's lost through endless months spent inside

The White Horse, Edwarstone, Suffolk

Little Earth Project is one of the most exciting breweries in the country. Using local ingredients, oak barrels and a house yeast derived from the owners' cider business, they make wild beers inspired by historic recipes. You can drink Barley Wines, Saisons and IPAs as they might have tasted 200 years ago. And since they took over the pub next door, you can do it in a place every bit as old.

Little Earth is in a dark wood barn tucked behind the historic White Horse. The beautiful red-brick building and character of its oak beams, blackboards and bric-a-brac are reflected in the local customers. You'll get a top-notch pint of Crouch Vale Brewers Gold and often a great Lager from Braybrooke, but with Little Earth next door this is really a haven for wild fermentation fans. You'll find several taps of their unique fruited and sour Saisons, all fermented using their house culture and probably some very old barrels. On top of that you'll find a fridge full of the brewery's bigger beers and rarities from the UK's other wild drinks producers including Mills, Burning Sky and Oliver's Cider.

Whatever you're drinking you can take it out to the beer garden, which buzzes with bees busily flitting about the flowers and fruits that grow around it, as well as the barking of dogs and the shouts of their excited beer geek owners. It feels about as close to nature as you can get while still on a licensed premises. There's a few self-catering lodges and a campsite, too, so you don't have to worry about driving home if you don't want to. Instead, you can wake up in a hot tent, and crawl out in search of water and a cool breeze after a night of sharing one too many bottles.

Falmouth Harbour, Cornwall

I'm not certain about the legalities and etiquette of this recommendation, but I have gotten away with it on multiple occasions. The harbourside right behind the high street is home to several great venues. The first is the Chain Locker, a St Austell pub serving bang-fresh Proper Job and doorstep crab sandwiches with tables right up to the water. If you're hankering for some traditional fish and chips then Harbour Lights does amazing freshly cooked cod and haddock, and is above a local favourite, the Front. This pub seems to be happy for you to bring in food from upstairs, so long as you slake your thirst with copious amounts of cask – my recommendation is Skinner's Lushingtons, which is a beautiful Cascade Pale Ale. If you've had your fill of fish, the Stable next door does decent Roman-style pizza and has an excellent real cider range you can enjoy on its terrace. And finally, if you're happy to break rather than bend the rules, you can pick up some cans and small plates from Verdant's wonderful Seafood Bar, then tuck into it with your legs dangling off the harbour walls. Just watch out for police ... and seagulls.

By the River Brew Co, Newcastle

Drinking under a bridge has never been an aspiration of mine, but there's no denying the joy of doing it under such an iconic one, especially when you are drinking beer as good as By the River's. Depending on where you sit, the aroma is accompanied by some other incredible smells – smoked and barbecued meats,

freshly cooked pizza dough, warm burritos and more. By the River is not just a brewery, it's a tiny shipping container city with beer at its heart. It's owned by the same folk who own Wylam Brewery, and the beer is equally as delicious. The place is no suntrap, however, so I think it's at its best enjoyed at dusk as the lights come on around you and on the other side of the Tyne.

Newcastle is actually spoiled for wonderful outdoor drinking spots. If you're planning to spend the evening at By the River, you could do a lot worse than taking during the day to visit one of the UK's best pubs, the Free Trade Inn, which just happens to have a killer view across the city. You're also only a short drive from one of the UK's most idyllic rural taprooms – head 40 minutes north to Morpeth for the hairy cows, barns and open fields of Rigg & Furrow Brewery.

Rivington Brewing Co Tap, Chorley, Lancashire

Found less than an hour outside the craft beer hub of Manchester, Rivington Brewing Co needed to build something special to coax people out – and they have done exactly that. The taproom has a practical but very natural feel, with the tables made from wooden boards and casks, oil drums and even old tractor tyres, looking out over the canopy of the tree-decked hills. An early focus on building a local community has allowed the brewers to make pretty much anything they want, so the tap list will vary with everything from Grisettes to Pastry Stouts. In fact, the tap and can list is usually so impressive I'd advise staying at the on-site caravan and camping field so you can either go late into the night or have another crack at it the next day.

Fyne Ales, Cairndow, Argyll

Fyne Ales sits in the basin of a valley, right at the head of Loch Fyne. Just writing that sentence makes me want to visit, but it's the sense of peace and incredible views that really sell it. You truly will feel at the heart of the 450 acre farm that the brewery is set in, as well as part of the beautiful natural surroundings.

If you come for the location, you'll still end up staying for the beers. Fyne's flagship beer, Jarl, is one of the best cask beers in the UK. I love its unusual expression of Citra, which creates prickly berry, elderflower and citrus peel at a very sessionable 3.8%. Jarl is the perfect reward for a day spent hiking up the Bens, but the best beer to drink while visiting Fyne is Home. This three-year blend of spontaneous barrel-aged wild ales is made using local malts and water, as well as the indigenous yeasts of the valley. It's a true taste of the region.

King Street, Bristol

If you're looking for the world's most convenient pub crawl, or trying to find the place in the UK with the most free-of-tie taps per square mile, then you need to head to King Street. This cobbled and pub-lined road is a beautiful site on a summer's day, with people spilling out and retaking the streets in the name of great beer. You can get your serious niche beer from Small Bar; a wide variety of pintable kegs and cask from the cavernous Royal Navy Volunteer (as well as excellent food); shelter from the sun in the cellars of the Beer Emporium; or grab an outside table

for some King Street Brewhouse beers – several of which are made on site. If you're more of a cider drinker there's the beer garden and canal barge that forms the Apple. The drinks list is a little safe, but there are gems to be found from local producers.

Finally, if all that drinking threatens to get too much, then just a few metres up the canal is Three Brothers Burgers, which combines borderline filthy burgers with a beer bottle list the length of your arm.

Little Pomona Taproom (and the Yew Tree Inn), Herefordshire

My eureka moment with craft beer happened so long ago that it's hard to separate the reality from the myth. But my memory of the time my head was turned by cider is crystal clear, and it was a glass of Little Pomona's Do It Puritan 2019 at their taproom in Herefordshire. It's a joyful place to spend a Saturday at any time of year, but a few sunny hours drinking natural cider among the apple trees can't be beaten. The cidery is found on the Brookhouse hop farm, so you can also head down in September to witness (from a distance) the comings and goings on the hop harvest – as well as see the first pressings of the orchard harvest. Ask co-founder Susanna Forbes for more tips on where to drink cider locally and she will insist you head to Ross-on-Wye Cider's Yew Tree Inn, a beautiful old pub with a dedicated cider shop and large garden for drinking in.

But the
sun
melts
away

August

We don't really associate August with the harvest. It seems too early, but in barley terms the hour is getting late. The grassy shoots of May have grown through the green stalk stage to become beautiful ears of barley that create fields of gold, moving like sun reflected on the sea. As the ears get too heavy they stop pointing to the sky and arch back down to earth, the sign that they are ready for harvest. In just a matter of weeks they will all be cut down, and the fields will be bare once again. Of course, that's not the end of the journey – the grains must be germinated and kilned to be ready to brew, a remarkable process that's taken centuries to perfect.

While that's happening at the top of the supply chain, August plays host to the two biggest beer festivals in the UK – both alike in dignity, but very different in approach. Centuries ago we would have been drinking through the last of that year's winter beers and praying for a good harvest to help with the next vintage, and even today there is a sense of anticipation. That's the only way I can explain why IPA Day falls in August, a truly unseasonable time to celebrate these big, hoppy beers. For me, August is a time for sipping shandies after mowing the lawn, steady Pale Ale sessions in pub gardens, and stubbies by the barbecue. I'll save the serious, adventurous drinking for autumn and winter, just around the corner.

What to drink

At beer festivals all the rules are thrown out, but in between those heady hours with a sampling glass you might find some early releases of Märzens and Festbier, which are great to graduate to in the evening after a few lighter Helles or Pilsners. You might also find the first of the wild ales made during the abundance of spring: unless it's spending lots of time in barrel, three or four months is about right for a wild ale to come to fruition. Of course, if a heatwave comes then you might be reaching for a shandy or two – just make sure the lemonade is as good as the beer you mix it with.

What to eat

Wild raspberries are really singing around this time of year, which means a lot of breweries will be foraging for them, but probably won't release the beers until September and October. In the meantime, though, you can pick them for crumbles and pies, or to add to your own homebrews. Potatoes are also a big August crop, just in time for the incredible amount of chips eaten during Oktoberfest. Finally, August is perhaps the most fertile time for fish, and there is lots of seasonal and delicious seafood to be found – crab, mackerel, langoustines and more if you're by the seaside or have a great local fishmonger.

Where to go

There are so many beer festivals and events it's hard to know where to start, but the Great British Beer Festival is the biggest celebration of cask ale in the world and (especially if you can go on one of the earlier days) you'll find an incredible range of beer in great condition. London Craft Beer Festival is the UK's biggest 'craft' beer festival in the UK, and as such brings an impossible range of styles under one roof (although technically most of it is open air). Sheffield Indie Beer Feast is also well worth a visit – the city is probably the UK's most underrated beer and pub destination for both modern and traditional brewing.

Finally, it's Bristol's Cider Salon, a week-long celebration of great cider hosted by some of the most important figures in the industry, including none other than Tom Oliver.

If a **heatwave** comes then you might be reaching for a **shandy or two** – just make sure the lemonade is as good as the beer you mix it with

The barley harvest

Beer begins at the farm

The rise of American-style brewing means even traditional real ale brewers now use hops from the Pacific North-West for many of their beers. But whether you're a centuries-old ale brewer or a new hype IPA factory, you're likely to use exclusively British malt.

I'm not just talking about UK breweries either. Such is our reputation for malted barley that brewers all over the world choose to import our malt rather than use local varieties. I was amazed to see sacks of Thomas Fawcett & Sons at the seminal Alchemist Brewery in Vermont, and piles of Simpsons Malt at Garage Brew Co in Barcelona. And yet it took a trip to Crisp Malt's Norfolk outpost, in the quaint Norfolk village of Great Ryburgh, to hammer home how Britain's barley and malting techniques are the nation's greatest contribution to global brewing. We've already seen how our technology helped change European brewing in the 1800s, but our influence and reputation continues to this day.

Founded in 1870, Crisp is now a fascinating contrast of chrome and rusted iron equipment; of modern thinking and historic techniques. The floor malting room has been there since the start. More than 150 grain harvests have left deep grooves and scars in the stone floor, and weathered the original oak beams and steel posts, made just a few hundred metres away in the village. Around this historic site is a maze of new buildings, built up and around the original two malting floors to include cutting-edge technology like the stories-high tower kilns that roast Crisp's speciality malts.

I visited in late July, just as harvest was about to begin, and the sense of anticipation was palpable. This usually starts weeks earlier, but heavy rain meant the crops were still too wet to harvest, and could rot if cut and stored. Everyone had been praying for a run of hot, sunny days to dry it out and finish off the maturation, but there was no sign of one. There's still plenty of grain to be malted as the end of last year's harvest works its way through the plant, but the weighing bridge, where the deliveries head first to be tested and approved, was oddly quiet. Harvest has two peaks – in mid-July when the winter-sown malt is cut, and early August when the spring varieties come in. At those times Crisp can take up to 60 deliveries a day

Such is our reputation for **malted barley** that brewers **all over the world** choose to import our malt rather than use local varieties

(that's one every 10 minutes), but for now it's just a trickle of lorries coming through.

When we talk about different malts we only really talk about how they've been kilned – the process that results in Pilsner malt, pale malt, caramalt, chocolate malt – rather than the varieties themselves, but the lorries bring in a wide array of different grains. That could be wheat, oats or even rye, but most of it will be barley. Most of what comes through Crisp is Planet, a spring variety known for its consistency and efficiency, but the maltster also deals with a huge amount of Maris Otter. Created in the 1960s by cross-breeding two other varieties, this beautiful grain yields a lot less than Planet, but is loaded with biscuity flavour that makes it a favourite with traditional British brewers.

Once it passes tests for nitrogen and contaminants at the weighing bridge, the grain is stored at controlled temperature and moisture levels until needed. Pretty much all the grains go through the two systems of the main plant, controlled from a central room. The first step is to steep the grain in warm water, which simulates the feeling of being in the wet earth and encourages the seeds to germinate and grow. That starts to release the starches that would give it energy to grow into a plant, but just as importantly makes them accessible to brewers during the mash. The malt is then laid on grates that push moist, warm air through the bed to keep conditions ideal for germination. That process takes up to four days, after which the grain is kilned for a little over 24 hours to dry out and add some colour and flavour. The temperature of that kilning process is what determines the kind of malt produced – staying as low as 55°C for Pilsner and Pale malts, but rising to at least double that for

Chocolate and Black malts. Those more specialist malts go through Crisp's bizarre vertical kilns, the only ones of their kind in the UK. These two ribbed towers vibrate like old washing machines, making the malt dance inside them to ensure an even roast on all sides.

On the big plant, the whole process takes around eight days, but back in the historic floor malting room, things take a little longer. With just a line of air conditioning vents to influence temperature and moisture, floor germination takes a few more days and lots more manual labour to turn the grain. On top of that, kilning usually takes around three days to reach the right colour, flavour and moisture content. During the drive for efficiency in the post-war period, this was a problem that needed to be solved and resulted in the technology of the main plant. The naturally slower process of floor malting, however, means a richer and more complex malt flavour in the final beer. Letting nature go at its own pace, then essentially slow-cooking the grain leaves the more delicate flavour compounds intact, which means floor malt is in great demand from brewers who appreciate the traditional methods or see enough flavour difference to swallow the extra cost.

Letting **nature go at its own pace,** then essentially slow-cooking the grain leaves the **more delicate flavour compounds** intact

Most of those brewers will be making beer where the malt makes up most of the character – likely English and central European styles. Crisp recently brought back a heritage barley called Haná, which was the malt used in the original Pilsner Urquell beers back in the mid-1800s. It's a hard grain to grow, with a low yield and a tendency to fall over in heavy rain (which is exactly what 2021 has brought) but with the harvest happening late I was able to visit one of just four Haná fields in the UK. As a Pilsner obsessive it was a very exciting moment, but it was slightly tempered by the sight that greeted me. Around half the field was horizontal, sagging under the heavy heads of grain that had been battered into submission by torrential downpours. As we walked around surveying the damage, technical director Dr Dave Griggs muttered that 'this is exactly why no one grows heritage grain'. Perhaps seeing my reaction, he assured me the grain was still perfectly harvestable, but would take longer to mature and dry out.

Patience is always rewarded in beer, however. It's taken seven years for Crisp to get to the point of releasing it but Haná's depth is extraordinary, providing a level of brioche, digestive biscuit and caramel that I thought was only achievable by decoction or a heavier kilned malt. The benefits and possibilities are clear, especially to the new guard of Lager brewers in the UK. Lost and Grounded, makers of the seminal Kellerpils, are already excited about the possibilities. Usually head brewer Alex Tronscoso only uses continental Pilsner malts, but the chance to use a British variety was too good to pass up. Their first trial of it, a rustic hoppy Lager called Newstalgic, surprised everyone (brewer included) with its rich malt character that perfectly balanced a heavy hit of Target, Challenger and Goldings from Kent's Hukin's Hops.

Crisp has also brought back a historic British barley malt called Chevallier, which was the dominant variety during the brewing boom of the 1800s and would have appeared in both Milds and Porters. As we've discussed, many breweries bought cheaply processed malts to save on money and tax, but doing so meant they missed out on the beautiful flavours of Chevalier when properly cared for. Crisp advertises it as 'Maris Otter turned up to 11', and it is remarkably biscuity, but it also has a kind of marmalade bitterness to it once in the beer, adding fruity depth to anything from Bitters to modern West Coast IPAs. The Cheshire Brewhouse has a whole line of beers made using old recipes found in brewing archives, and head brewer Shane Swindells' Gibralter Porter is loaded with this pithy, biscuity malt. At an eyebrow-raising 8.1% it's not a beer I'd advise for this time of year, but the layers of Hovis biscuit, Schwarzbrot and orange peel-like flavours is unlike any Porter I've had before.

The revival of so many brewing styles has been a huge blessing for maltsters like Crisp. Most of their volume still goes to distillers and macro Lager brewers, but the craft beer revolution has allowed them to invest in their speciality malt production, and to build better relationships with farmers based on quality rather than quantity. The fact that some have been willing to risk these heritage varieties proves that, as farmers have to be, they are willing to go where the wind takes them. Dr Griggs says the last few years have seen a real drive towards flavour and variety rather than efficiency and consistency, something Crisp has tried to both anticipate and foster.

As with all elements of beer production, we've spent the last two centuries trying to iron out the kinks of seasonality in barley farming. Cross-breeding and selection programmes mean the barley used today is incredibly reliable, and a few week's delay to harvest is about as bad as it gets. But as global warming gives us longer, wetter periods and new temperature records every year, it's not getting easier, whether you're growing heritage or modern grains. Even so, there will never be much seasonality to the output of large maltsters. They can store enough grain to keep malting all year round and supply their breweries with whatever malt they need regardless. Even though malt production is almost seasonless, its use in beer production definitely evolves throughout the year. In fact, malt is the ingredient most changed as the seasons continue their endless cycle – the amounts mashed in, the colours chosen, and the proportions used. The shade of the beers reflects the length of the days, and the strengths go up as the temperatures go down.

Malt really is the key to seasonality in brewing, and everything springs from that base. The wider the colours and varieties that maltsters produce, the more brewers can respond to and be inspired by their surroundings. Drinking a can of Newstalgic in the field of Haná was the distillation of everything I've written about in this book – forging a connection between what's in the glass, what went into making it, and where and when it's enjoyed.

IPA Day

Not that we needed one

For many craft beer drinkers, every day is IPA day. Such is our affection for hop-forward, strong blond beer that every time we get bored of it, rather than find a new style to obsess over we simply invent a new variant.

Our lupulin-fuelled tunnel vision has resulted in an ever-growing list of different IPAs, including West Coast IPA, New England IPA, English IPA, Black IPA, Red IPA, Brut IPA, Cold IPA, Mountain IPA, Belgian IPA, Sour IPA and IPL. Within all of those substyles you'll find sub-substyles that designate the strength: Micro IPA, Session IPA, Double IPA, Triple IPA and Quadruple IPA. In fact, at this point IPA has come to mean anything you'd regard as overtly hop-forward. It's as much a marketing term as it is a style designation, used to ensure sales where breweries fear that using another name might not whip up the same level of hype.

These styles are all, of course, a far cry from the hoppy, well-aged amber-coloured ales that would have been sent to India in the 19th century. Even then, though, the term was a marketing ploy, being sold in the UK at least as 'Pale Ale, as prepared for India' to both differentiate it and add some mystery and glamour. In truth, the only thing that changed was a significantly heavier dry hop, which helped preserve the beer on its long journey … as well as the price. Back then IPA was much less popular than Porter, and remained a niche style right through the reigns of Mild, Bitter and Pilsner. Today it's still only popular within the geeky niche, but boy does it dominate it. In the craft beer scene IPA now plays the role that Pale

Lager does outside of it: the everyday drink that offers an escape from the anxiety of choice.

So if we're drinking IPAs most days, it's legitimate to wonder why there's a specific IPA Day at all. A more interesting question for this book, however, is why – of all the months of the year – was August picked? For a start, hops are harvested in September, meaning the IPAs drunk on the day will be as stale as they could possibly be. Secondly, for the northern hemisphere, where most of the hops are grown and most IPAs are made, it's the height of summer – the time of year where reaching for a 7% beer risks you falling asleep in the sun and waking up the colour of a Red IPA. Finally, the majority of IPAs made these days sway towards the New England style, which is sweeter, fuller and less bitter – all characteristics that encourage slow sipping and bottle sharing, rather than crushing full cans and reaching into the cooler for another, as I tend to do on an August weekend.

Thankfully, the endless expansion of the India Pale Ale empire means we can adjust our IPA choices according to the time of year, offering up a hop-forward beer

for all occasions and moods. On IPA Day I'll be reaching for Session- and Mountain-style IPAs, which retain a crisp finish and light, grainy body. Thornbridge is fantastic at these more refreshing hazy beers, and four-packs of Green Mountain and Jamestown are the best hoppy fridge fillers this time of year, if I can find the space between countless 500ml cans of DEYA Steady Rolling Man. I also enjoy Jaipur in summer as well, though I like to serve them frostier than I would an IPA in autumn, when I generally switch to the maltier but still zippy and refreshing West Coast styles. Sadly, the pressure to increase the juice factor in brewing has made bright and raspingly bitter IPA a rarity in the UK, but breweries like Abbeydale, Burnt Mill, Black Iris and North Brew Co all regularly make great examples.

Winter already sees a glut of Black IPAs come out, as hop-loving brewers look across the bar to see an abundance of Porters, Stouts, Quads and Dubbels. Untappd has recorded a spike of this famously divisive style in January for the last few years, showing it is very much a winter IPA. The best of them avoid overt roastiness, instead using the dehusked carafe malts found in German Dark Lagers to achieve treacle-like decadent sweetness and notes of milk chocolate that suit the citrusy hops far better. If that sounds a little too radical for your palate, Red IPAs are a great autumn and winter alternative, offering that big piney West Coast hit but also rich toffee, dark caramel and dried fruit notes. The best place to get both these styles is an industrial estate near Wokingham, where neighbours Siren and Elusive are still trying desperately to make them cool.

For me spring and early summer are the time for New England IPAs. Not only is this when the fresh American hops reach our shores, but they glow like the first

Thornbridge is fantastic at these **more refreshing hazy beers**, and four-packs of Green Mountain and Jamestown are the best **hoppy** fridge fillers

sunny days, and are abundant with juicy fruit esters and tangy tropical top notes. Intense Double IPAs are great for festivals and nights with friends where you can share, but the sweet spot for intensity and drinkability with these styles is around 6.5% – the strength of pretty much all Verdant's IPAs, including the incredible Even Sharks Need Water. This beautiful beer ranks among some of the very best New England IPAs made in the States, and is a riot of apricot yeast esters and dankly overripe mango from the Citra, Simcoe and Galaxy. The latter hop also adds a hint of wild, untamable bitterness that stops it ever becoming cloying.

It's hard to explain quite why IPA has become such a dominant cultural force in craft beer. In truth, the variation within it is so wild you could quite happily only drink beers labelled as such and still adapt to meet all the seasons. The one thing I do know is that you'll find that hardest in August, so let's make every day IPA Day.

Oh wait, that's right. We already have.

Britain's great beer festivals

Our best chance to explore

You can learn a lot at a beer festival if you remember it all. There are, of course, inherent risks in offering endless samples of strong beer in a party atmosphere, but generally for me a festival isn't about inebriation.

Don't get me wrong, there is a lot of fun to be had, but festivals are the ultimate opportunity to explore and learn about the beer scene. To me, drinking in a pub is all about finding a beer you love on top form, and drinking that by the pint until you leave. At a festival, though, I'll rarely go back for the same thing twice. Where else could you follow a historic Mild with a Pastry Stout, cleanse your palate with a clean Berliner Weisse, then try a series of single-hopped Double IPAs? What's more, the small pour format most beer festivals have adopted takes away the fear that you might not like a new style or brewery, letting you escape your own expectations for once.

There are now UK beer festivals all year around, and our startlingly diverse brewing scene means each one can serve entirely different beer from entirely different breweries. The events themselves are as varied as the beers they champion, too. I've been to ones held in castles, nature reserves, old swimming baths, remote fields and, of course, giant London Expo centres. The best events are those where all our cultures clash – adjunct-laden keg beer next to cask bitter, trendy street food next to a sausage roll guy, socks and sandals next to Converse and skinny jeans. Beer should be the great leveller.

Although the craft beer scene as a whole still fails to represent the UK's diverse population, our festivals are at the forefront of changing that. There are few who can resist the idea of a beer festival, and the increasing attempts to bring other scenes and industries in has introduced thousands of new people, whether it's from the worlds of wine, coffee, music, art or even literature.

One of the best events at doing that is London Craft Beer Festival (LCBF). Held on the first full weekend of August at the iconic Tobacco Dock, well over 10,000

The best events are those where all our **cultures clash** – adjunct-laden keg beer next to cask bitter, **trendy street food** next to a **sausage roll guy**, socks and sandals next to Converse and skinny jeans

THE KERNEL BREWERY

- PALE ALE SIMCOE 5.5%
- BIERE DE SAISON NELSON SAUVIN 5.1%
- TABLE BEER CITRA TETTNANGER 2.9%
- DRY STOUT CENTENNIAL COLUMBUS 4.6%

people come through doors – and many of them aren't beer geeks at all. Joining the 50 or so breweries are wine makers, distillers and soda jerks, as well as famous DJs and some of the country's most distinguished chefs. Craft beer really struggles to find a place in fine dining restaurants, which makes this event perhaps the only place to enjoy some of the best beer in the world with food from the likes of 10 Greek Street, Brigadiers, the Palomar, Berber & Que and Two Lights. By bringing these different scenes together LCBF transcends the traditional bubble that beer festivals exist in. Beer is everywhere in daily life and a central part of our culture, which means it doesn't exist in a vacuum. All good festivals will echo that in how they are put together.

But LCBF isn't the only big beer event that happens in the capital this August weekend. Over on the other side of town at the Kensington Olympia is the largest cask ale celebration in the world – the Great British Beer Festival. Run by CAMRA itself, GBBF's reputation has very much mirrored the organisation and has gone through ebbs and flows of relevance and irrelevance.

It was first held in 1975 at the old flower market in Covent Garden. Unlike the well-drilled event we know now, by all accounts it was absolute chaos. Just days beforehand it was discovered that the venue didn't have an alcohol licence (luckily Fuller's stepped in to help) and according to one of the organisers 'all hell broke loose' when the doors finally opened. Queues to get in went around the block, there wasn't enough glassware, many paying customers had to be drafted in to serve beer (until that ran out too), and at some point half the takings were stolen. Despite that, such incredible interest in the event assured CAMRA it was worth doing again – both to raise funds for the organisation and as a very effective campaigning tool.

When I first went in 2010 I was struck by how samey the beer was, and the advanced age of those drinking with me. Since then, however, I've seen a steady shift in both. The variety of British-brewed cask has rocketed in the last decade, as has the quality – especially if you can go at the start of the week when the selection is at its widest and freshest. The addition of the American and European beer stands has been an inspiration, and wonderfully makes GBBF one of the most likely places to find niche German Pilsner and bottles or even boxes of rare Lambic. As a result of all this, the crowds that attend are starting to diversify and make the event feel more in touch with the ever-changing world around it.

In terms of relevance, of course, it has never been more important. Gone are the days when a cask festival could create the kind of scene witnessed at Covent Garden, and cask beer has been in volume – if not cultural – decline for nearly a decade now. That puts extra pressure on cask festivals and indeed CAMRA itself to make sure that new people are discovering the joys of real ale. There has been a lot of pressure for GBBF to modernise its beer selection further, but I'm glad they resist. Together with LCBF, this usually hot and muggy weekend is one of my favourites in the beer calendar. They complement and contrast with each other so well, and as the amount of people that attend both grows, our beer scene starts to look richer and richer.

Beer shandies

The ultimate form of refreshment

Shandies get a bad rep. We've spent decades seeing them as the lighter option: the compromise if you're driving, the lunchtime concession, the hot day salvation. It all comes from the entirely flawed idea that mixing our beer with … well, anything … is just watering it down. But there's no clear reason why. Spirit producers spend most of their time convincing people to mix their drinks – a little water in your Scotch, some Vermouth with your vodka – while beer drinkers consider it sacrilege.

It's ahistorical for many reasons. For a start, blending is and always has been a natural part of the brewing process. We sometimes liquor back strong worts to get a lower ABV; we mix two batches of IPA to get consistency; we blend different ages of Lambic to make Gueuze. More recently, styles like the Triple Fruited Gose are celebrated for being as much fruit pulp as sour beer, so why do we suddenly consider it beneath us to blend with the final product? What's more is that shandies themselves have a rich history, with the original term 'Shandygaff' appearing in the early 19th century. Charles Dickens even mentions it, although back then it would have likely been a blend of alcoholic ginger ale and Porter.

Perhaps it speaks to the slightly erroneous connection we have made between the strength of a beer and its quality. It's something we likely learned from our historic brewing scene, when bigger beers had to have expensive malts and longer maturing time to reach those ABVs. But today that's not the case, and anyone who has drunk Tennents Super can attest to the fact that bigger is not always better.

The important mental leap to make is to think of shandies as adding to beer, rather than taking away. Once you frame as such, there are all kinds of exciting combinations that accentuate, balance or contrast beer flavours to make something entirely different but no worse than the original two ingredients.

As usual, when it comes to beer culture, the Germans are well ahead of us. Not only do they regularly add lemonade to their Lagers – they call it a *'radler'* or 'cyclist' beer – they use all sorts of other flavours. Head backstage at a craft beer festival in Europe and it's pretty likely you'll see hungover brewers trying to get back into the swing of things with a 'Schoff', or Schofferhofer Grapefruit. This beautiful shandy is a combination of Schofferhofer's Hefeweizen and grapefruit soda, and it's hard to think of something more reviving if you've got to keep the party going.

The real joy of shandies, however, is inventing your own. Especially if, like me, you take great joy in committing some serious crimes against craft. As a kid I used to spend hours making silly cocktails with our old SodaStream, and that love of crashing big flavours together has stayed with me long into adulthood. One of my favourite shandies of all time is the 50/50 combination of Lilt and Saison Dupont – the dryness of the Saison balances the overly sweet soda, and adds spicy aromas and bready depth to make something entirely new and crushable.

My greatest creation, however, is 60/30 blend of a hoppy kettle sour and Coke. It sounds mad until you relate it to one of the greatest penny sweets of all time – the fizzy cola bottle. The sherbet fizz comes from the tart beer and hoppy hit, while the Coke creates a base of sweet caramel. The first sip is like being dragged back to filling your paper bag at the Pick'n'Mix stand at Woolworths.

If you're looking for a proper hop hit at a low ABV, grapefruit and orange sodas can really work with New England IPAs. The flavour profiles are pretty similar, but the acidity of the soda cuts through the sweet, thick beer to add tartness and bite. It's totally tailorable too: a splash simply brightens up the beer, while an equal blend changes it completely into a refreshing fruit salad, best served at absolute zero on a fiercely hot day.

Dark beers can make beautiful shandies too, but require some more traditional British sodas to work. The addition of 25% old-school Dandelion & Burdock can bring a slightly dull Porter to life, as well as giving it a more aromatic and summery feel. If you want something a little more wintery, a properly spicy ginger ale is great with both Porter and Stout – much like Charles Dickens might have enjoyed.

Of course, little can beat the classic lemonade and Lager. There's a lot to be said for a trashy Lager and a good glug of Schweppes when the mercury is nearly coming out the top of the thermometer, but upgrading both is always going to be better. In particular I'd recommend a soda made with high-quality lemons. Square Root uses all Amalfi lemons, freshly squeezed and zested into a sugar syrup then carbonated to make a gloriously sticky, tart lemonade that adds complexity to all Lagers, good and bad. Helles make the best shandies thanks to their low bitterness and rich, malty bodies, but whatever is in the fridge will do at a pinch. If you're using something lighter like a macro Lager, just lower the lemonade content from 50% to 30% and you'll have a beautiful summer drink.

If you really want to annoy your beer snob friends, put a garnish in it too – lemon is good, lime is better. The only addition I can't condone is ice, which will water down the cocktail and knock out the carbonation much quicker than just a glass that's been in the fridge for 30 minutes. Otherwise, when it comes to the greatest form of refreshment on earth, there are no rules.

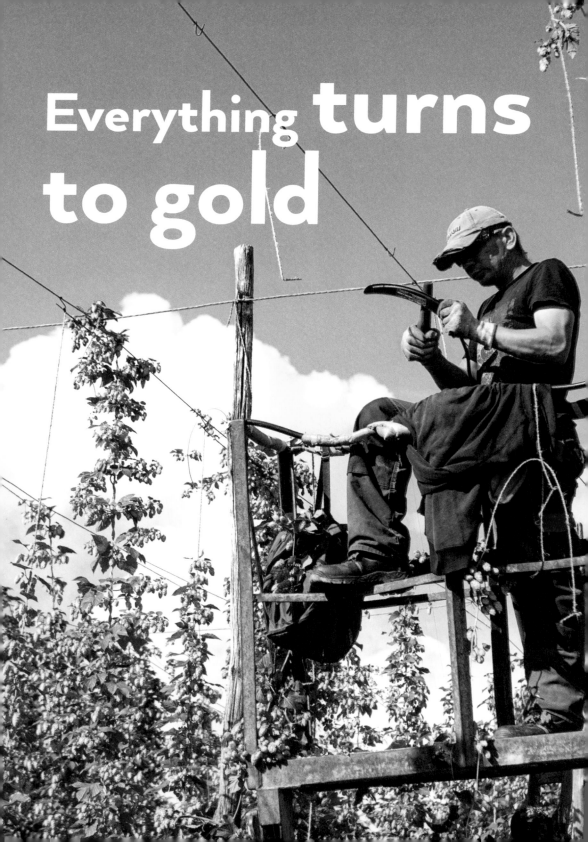

Everything **turns to gold**

September

For many, the end of summer is something to be lamented. The days get colder, the evenings shorter, our clothes heavier. But for me, the start of autumn is a magical time. The fresh snap of the morning, the golden sun lounging lower in the sky, the warmth of winter coats we haven't worn for months.

For beer geeks there is no better time of year. Not only is there the chance of my first fireside ale, there's also the greatest beer festival of all – Oktoberfest – and the glut of caramel-tinged Festbiers that comes with it. I'm yet to find a British version of Oktoberfest that reaches the euphoric highs of the beer, food and family festival held in Munich each year, but for now, having the official imported beers and the increasingly excellent British varieties transports me.

We still have those stolen moments in beer gardens, too, where a flashback of summer combines with the low light and red leaves. If I'm really lucky I'll be able to enjoy a pint with green hops from this year's harvest at the same time. These beers are made using hops fresh off the bine, carrying unique flavours from field to glass and giving us a hint of what's in store from that year's vintage.

In the 19th century the UK was one of the biggest hop producers in the world, but today our farms are in a state of flux, fighting issues such as global warming and Brexit as they wrestle to get their share of the limelight in the new craft beer world. While many beer geeks dismiss native UK varieties like Fuggles, Goldings and Bramling Cross as boring, there are still millions all over the world who revere their subtle, spicy and bramble notes, and who understand how centuries of using them together with British malt and yeast has created a unique brewing culture that deserves our attention as much as any American-inspired approach.

No time of year better underlines the exciting, diverse nature of British brewing – from green-hopped cask ales to long-matured Lagers, via modern IPAs made with freshly landed New Zealand hops, and mixed fermentation beers made with spring and summer's best ingredients. Autumn isn't just the end of summer – it's the start of beer season.

What to drink

As the light turns amber so do many of the beers. Oktoberfest-style Lagers should start to hit the shelves, and these bittersweet German beers are perfect for late-summer garden sipping. Lost and Grounded's Forest Drift is utterly brilliant and traditional, while Donzoko's Festbier is a little lighter and more floral. You can't go wrong with the real thing either – only six breweries are allowed to pour at Munich's Oktoberfest, and all of them make beautiful (if very similar) beers for the occasion. Hacker-Pschorr and Paulaner's beers are usually available in good bottleshops and supermarkets while the Festbiers from Spaten, Augustiner, Hofbräu and Löwenbräu can be found on beer-by-mail sites.

Finally, but perhaps most importantly, late September to early October is the only time of year in the UK when you can get your hands on green hop beers. Made using freshly picked hops (rather than the usual dried ones), they bring new complexity to classic British-style beers – think white grape floralness, fresh grass and prickly bramble.

What to eat

It's the season of root veg abundance, so get hold of everything you can that says 'Grown in the UK', roast it with oil, herbs and garlic, then serve with… well, anything else seasonal. The malty German-style Lagers of this time of year and the fresh hop British ales are perfect with autumnal vegetables and also both ideal if you are inspired by the flavours of Oktoberfest – rotisserie chicken, roast pork, braised cabbage and pretzels.

Where to go

September is a manic month for beer festivals. There are so many Oktoberfests happening around the country that knowing which are legit and which are just a few flags and a rebadged Lager is hard. My tips are to only go to those serving locally made beer or one of the six official Oktoberfest breweries – that way you'll at least have an exciting drinking experience and can simply request Robbie Williams 'Angels' for a taste of the real thing. I'll explain later.

Kent is the place to be otherwise, with several green hop festivals, tap takeovers and parades. Some feel a little too Wickerman for my liking, but the beer is usually fresh and excellent, and they make a fantastic family day out.

If you're looking for something a little craftier, the Leeds International Beer Festival falls in September too, and despite serving some world-class beer it doesn't take itself too seriously.

Malty **German-style Lagers** of this time of year and the fresh hop British ales are perfect with **autumnal vegetables**

The hop harvest

Gathering our green gold

For the pickers, the day starts at 4.30am. That's not when they get up, that's when they fire up the tractors and hitch a lift down to the fields. It's still summer technically, but you can see your breath at that time of morning and it mingles with the cigarettes many of the workers smoke to get a buzz.

There's not much conversation. Even if their voices weren't rusty from the beer, smokes and lack of sleep, the noise of the machinery means it's not worth the effort. Instead they focus on the task ahead: nearly twelve hours of Pacman-ing their way up and down each row of hops. One worker rides an articulated crane, cutting the bines from their wires with a small scythe, another waits at the bottom catching them, and a third trails behind to mop up what they miss. One tractor keeps them moving, while another two relay between the field and the farm, delivering each trailer-load of hops to the processing plant.

The work is incredibly hard and Ross Hukins, who owns the farm, relies on foreign labour. It's not because it's cheap – they will earn over £2,000 for three weeks' work – but because British people have proved unable to keep up with the pace. The only British workers in the fields are Ross's sister, who is driving one of the tractors, and a local chef who was made redundant after the COVID-19 lockdown. Ross says he got the job because he would be used 'to the long hours'.

The day I visit Hukins Hops the team is in good spirits. Yesterday it rained hard from start to finish, the pickers were soaked through and the land turned to mush. But today the sun is out in force, low in the sky and sepia-toned, but warm enough for t-shirts.

They marvel at the fact that anyone would come to photograph the process, let alone write about it. During the quick break where the tractors cut their engines, I'm asked so many questions I start to wonder who's actually doing the research. To them this is hard manual labour: the romance doesn't begin until it's turned into the beer I imagine they drink copious amounts of at the end of every day. I try to explain to them that, for me, this is the most exciting time of year. With malt there is still so much processing to do, but with the hops all that's needed is drying – and even that's not necessary to start brewing. This is a raw ingredient, thrown straight into the brew to kick out immediate flavours and aromas utterly unique to beer –

This is a **raw ingredient,** thrown straight into the brew to kick out **immediate flavours and aromas** utterly unique to beer aromas you can faintly catch on the wind a mile from the farm, and that you take home on your clothes when you leave. It's intoxicating. They smile and nod.

Back at the processing plant, work is relentless. After the hops are delivered to the loading bay, another team picks each individual bine and clips it to a conveyor that takes it up and away into a clanking iron machine that plucks the flowers. From there the hops are transported to the roof of the farmhouse and into gentle drying kilns, which reduce the moisture down to between 9% and 12%. Too low and you start to destroy the essential oils, too high and they could start to rot on the inside. Bizarrely, any rot actually causes a fire risk, because the hops are so tightly packed that the biological reaction generates enough heat to spontaneously combust.

The hops are then bailed and random samples cut out to ensure the quality. These hops are sold months in advance and have to last the year in storage, so making sure they are exactly to spec is vital. There is only one chance to pick and package hops right each year, and 2020 has been one of mixed fortunes. The quality is extremely high, but the hops themselves are much smaller than usual due to a wet spring. That means a lot less profit in a year where Ross took on significant debt to expand. He's betting on, and indeed campaigning for, much greater interest in British hops after decades of decline. The UK hop growing industry had all but disappeared by the late 1900s as large brewers switched to Continental hops. They didn't smell or taste any better, but they contained higher levels of the acids needed to add bitterness, and that meant the international Lager brewers could use a lot less. The result was devastation among the UK hop growing industry.

As the UK brewing industry exploded again a decade ago, there were hopes that the farms could recover. Unfortunately, the craft beer revolution was more interested

in the intense, aromatic and citric hops from the Pacific North-West of America. Beer geeks throughout the world, including British beer lovers, dismissed UK hops as dull and earthy – fine for traditional British brewing but not suited to the bigger, hoppier beers that were becoming so popular.

Hukins Hops is at the heart of changing that reputation, bringing heritage seed varieties back out of cold storage and growing them to experiment with. Already Ross is selling fields of Bullion, a hop originally used in Guinness but taken out of circulation decades ago. Guinness just used it for bittering, but when added at the end of the boil they burst with rich orange peel. Their aroma is only beaten by the sweet apricot notes from the Ernest hops, a variety that was abandoned by most growers decades ago due to its 'strong, coarse, American aroma'. If only they had known.

That's not to say that all British hops are going full-on Americana. Fuggles and Goldings will always dominate the harvest as they supply old customers and a small revolution in traditional brewing among the new guard. Breweries like DEYA Brewing Co, Northern Monk and BoxCar Brew Co made their name with ultra-modern American-style beers, but the founders have returned to the pints they drank while growing up. Served in can and on keg but remaining true to their recipe roots, they could introduce a new generation of drinkers to Bitter, ESB, Mild and Porter.

Most notable among them is Five Points Brewing Co, who quietly released their Best Bitter in 2019 as a passion project of head brewer Greg Hobbs but have struggled to brew enough ever since. They work closely with Ross, contracting all their British hops from him each year. Their Best Bitter is all Fuggles, but they also have another beer named Bullion – no prizes for guessing what hop that beer uses. Most excitingly though, the brewery has started hosting a green hop beer festival every October at their East London pub, the Pembury Tavern.

Green hops – also known as wet hops – are hops that aren't dried. Instead they go straight from the bine to the brewery, where they are tossed into the boil within hours of picking. There they add lots of aromas and flavours that are destroyed during the drying process, namely fresh grass, sweet resin and grape skin notes – exactly the aromas that hit you as you reach the hop farm.

Given the gorgeous and subtle flavours imparted by green hops, it's a wonder this seasonal tradition isn't more common among British brewers. Perhaps it's because green hop beers are notoriously hard to get right. The flowers need to be used the day they are picked, because the delicate oils start to decay from the moment they come off the bine. You also have to use significantly more to get the same level of flavour and aroma as they haven't been concentrated down. That's compounded by the fact that hops are sold by weight, so are much more expensive to buy green. In fact, Ross says if he could sell all his hops undried he'd be able to retire within a few years. Of course, he never would. This farm has been in his family for generations, and Ross Hukin has a lot more work to do.

Cask Ale Week

Keeping our brewing culture alive

If you'll forgive the pun, Cask Ale Week is a bittersweet time of year. On the one hand it's a celebration of one of the UK's greatest cultural and industrial traditions, a moment to reflect on how remarkable it is that this inefficient, unreliable but utterly joyful way of serving beer has survived the ravages of capitalism.

But the lack of engagement and excitement around it is also a reminder of how much work is needed to protect this heritage for future generations, who deserve their first pint of just-tapped cask ale. Because it's that beautiful moment that every passionate brewer, publican and beer geek knows can change someone's mind. Cask ale is the beer equivalent of freshly baked bread, still warm from the oven. There is this intangible moreishness to it, this full body and vital flavour that just seems to fade and go staler from that point on. It's still delicious – but those first few hours after tapping cannot be beaten as a beer-drinking experience.

That freshness is down to the fact that cask ale is sent to the pub unconditioned, possibly still fermenting gently in its cask to gain soft carbonation before being opened by the publican and rested until in perfect condition. It's therefore about as fresh as beer can get.

Its greatest strength, however, is also its greatest weakness – at its peak it's untouchable, but it falls so quickly from that peak that a lot of the cask ale poured in the UK is well past its best. I've lost count of the number of friends who have told me it tastes like vinegar, dishwater, twigs and feet – all classic signs of tired and oxidised beer at various states of decline. Often it's caused by pubs not keeping their cellars cool enough, or not cleaning their lines regularly enough, but the other major factor is the fact that not enough people are drinking it. While a keg of beer can easily last a week once tapped, a cask is pulling oxygen in as it empties, which stales the beer in a matter of days. If there aren't enough customers trying it to get through the cask in time, those who taste the end of the barrel are in for a rough experience. It's a Catch-22 situation – the beers will improve if more people drink it, but more people won't drink it unless the beers improve.

This is what makes Cask Ale Week so vital. With the cellars naturally cooler at this time of year, the average quality of cask ale coming out of the pumps rises a little and remains there until next summer. That makes now the perfect time for a national campaign that asks brewers to send out their freshest beer to pubs, encourages pubs to put fewer beers on and sell them fresh, and gets consumers out there to try special releases, green-hop beers and regional curiosities like the Hartlepool Head. The best thing we can do for cask ale is to encourage new people to try it, because the happy truth is that the more we drink of it, the fresher and better it gets – and the more we get through, the more chance we have of our tradition being around for future generations. So when Cask Ale Week comes around, try going to the pub with someone you know doesn't love cask ale. Try sharing some imagery and memories of it online. Ask your local breweries if there is anything you can do to help them get the message out. Oh, and drink lots of it.

Cask ale is the **lifeblood of our beer industry,** hidden in plain sight throughout our country

Because while cask ale is painted as bland and monochrome, or the preserve of the old and the sandalled, it's actually an incredibly diverse scene that few younger people have explored properly. You can have a juicy, fruity local Bitter in a village boozer in the Black Country, a citrusy and zingy Thornbridge Jaipur in a craft beer bar in Sheffield, a cask Mild in a mad micropub in Margate, or soft caramel and lemon-tinged Coniston Bluebird overlooking the Lakes. You can even enjoy a pint of Pride while waiting for your train at King's Cross Station. Cask ale is the lifeblood of our beer industry, hidden in plain sight throughout our country – we just need to guide people towards it.

Oktoberfest

It's not just about the beer

You know you're at an authentic Oktoberfest when Robbie William's hit 'Angels' comes on.

Hear me out. I've been to the Munich Oktoberfest twice in my life, both times getting a table at the Hacker-Pschorr tent. It's one of the biggest and most popular: an arena-sized drinking den with a bright blue roof decorated with clouds and the Hacker-Pschorr slogan – *Himmel der Bayern*, or 'the heaven of the Bayern people'. If you love sausages, beer, leather shorts, gingerbread, and desperately unfashionable 90s music then it lives up to the name.

You see, Oktoberfest isn't really a beer festival, and it never has been. It's actually a celebration of the kitsch side of Bavarian culture and, outside food, their tastes are quite particular. The fact that David Hasselhoff is something of a national hero is all you need to know, and Robbie Williams is not far behind. I'd estimate that 'Angels' – with its lilting, rousing chorus designed to be sung by slurring drunks – is played around once an hour in each tent. I am not exaggerating when I say it is a quintessential part of the festival. The anthem, even.

So I hold little regard for Oktoberfest celebrations that don't embrace the song, or at least the level of kitsch that it represents. Not all foreign Oktoberfests manage to balance the uninhibited joy with the focus on delicious food and beer. Like most local traditions that gain worldwide attention, there is plenty of misappropriation of culture – awful outfits, sexualisation, and plenty of cashing in. The result is a slightly jarring experience. Quingdao in China, for example, has one of the largest Oktoberfests outside of Germany, but the pole dancing and electro-music I witnessed there was not really in the spirit of things. The karaoke booths full of people singing 'Ironic' by Alanis Morrisette were much more in tune – well, some of it was.

Every year sees new British Oktoberfests added to the hundreds that already exist. They vary from simply putting a few of the official beers on tap and doing offers on hot dogs, to full-on marquees and litre Maß. Some are fantastic fun, but most miss the mark by not embracing the kitsch. When choosing which event to go to, you need to find a place that not only presents fantastic beer and food, but embraces the sheer cringe-worthiness of the original. I'm happy to report that I hadn't even finished my first pint at Lost and Grounded before 'Angels' played the first time.

Lost and Grounded is found in the industrial east of Bristol, about 30 minutes' walk down the canal from the centre. It's owned and run by Alex Tronscoso and Annie Clements, two Australians who settled in the UK after travelling the world. Alex had been a brewer back home in Perth, and after hoovering up lots of European brewing knowledge and drinking culture, decided to bring great German and Belgian staples to the UK. After some time as head brewer at Camden Town Brewery he created Lost and Grounded, which brews traditional Lagers and Belgian ales with one eye on the hop- and bitterness-loving British scene. Because of that, there's no UK brewery I'd trust more to make a crushable Oktoberfest-style beer (or to run an authentic event) than Lost and Grounded.

Of course, being 2020, Lost and Grounded couldn't recreate that riotous, table-dancing, Eurotrash atmosphere, but they nailed the beer. To be a true Oktoberfest beer the water must be pulled from the groundwater source underneath Munich, and only six breweries have the privilege of being allowed to pour there.

Made with mostly Munich malt, it has **rich biscuit and caramel notes,** cut through by tingly Mittelfruh hops that create an almost **liquorice-like tang**

However, technology means good breweries all over the world can now mimic that water profile, so they only have to worry about getting the malt, hops, yeast and process correct. Until the 1950s the official beer of Oktoberfest was the strong, hoppy, dark-copper Märzen. As I explained in the March chapter, these beers were replaced by the paler, less hoppy Festbier, which is essentially an extension of the breweries' core Helles beers.

Lost and Grounded's Festbier, Forest Drift, is higher carbonated than the official six Festbiers, as well as being a little darker and drier, perhaps in a nod to the original Märzen. Made with mostly Munich malt, it has rich biscuit and caramel notes, cut through by tingly Mittelfruh hops that create an almost liquorice-like tang. It glows in the light through the shutters as Lost and Grounded's bar staff carry the pints to people's tables. Despite being 5.6% it slips down disconcertingly easily, evidenced by the fact that most of the first round pints are replaced by litre Maß for the second. There's a pretty wide taplist, but no one is switching, their focus only occasionally broken to take mouthfuls of hot dog from the Airstream kitchen outside. There, two bearded men fry off giant *wurst* in between sips of beer, topping them with curried ketchup, mustard and crispy onions. Like the beers, they barely touch the sides.

To some extent it is strange that the world has started to appropriate this very German event, especially given the history of it. The first ever Oktoberfest was a party thrown for the townsfolk on the day that King Ludwig I married Princess Therese of Saxe-Hildburghausen, which creates the wonderful sense that you're crashing a wedding 200 years late. In a way, wherever it's held, Oktoberfest is still a marriage – of beer and the cultures that surround it. You just have to accept that Robbie Williams is the first dance.

Pretzels

The ultimate beer snack

A good pretzel is a dangerous thing. I'm not just talking about them being addictive and dry enough to make you drink at twice your normal pace – I'm talking about the dagger-like salt crystals that adorn them. In fact, if you don't get a cut on the roof of your mouth, then it wasn't a good pretzel.

I'm only partly joking. That big salty hit is vital, but so is the smooth and crunchy crust and pizza-dough centre. As a result, the only thing harder than making a proper German-style pretzel is finding one to buy, which is why I'm giving you this method. Of all the recipes in this book, this is the one that gave me the most trouble. Contrary to popular belief, the tying of the knot is actually the easy bit – lift and cross, cross again and drop. Done. The difficulties start long before then with the need to create a really airy dough in a very strange shape, and it finishes tricky too, with an alkali bath to get that signature thick crust.

It took me countless batches and a lot of carb comas to get this right, but I'm delighted to say I did manage to create the perfect accompaniment to a classic Festbier or Helles. One thing to note, however, is that these pretzels need to be consumed fast – after 24 hours that crust goes leathery, so make them on the day you're eating them and make sure you have plenty of friends (or appetite).

INGREDIENTS

1 x 7g pack of dry baking yeast

1 tablespoon of granulated sugar

Table salt

600g strong white bread flour

60g baking soda

Crystalised Sea Salt

METHOD

1 *Dissolve the yeast and sugar in 350ml of warm water and set aside. Sift the flour into a bowl and mix with a pinch of table salt, leaving a well in the middle. Slowly pour in the water and mix with a fork to combine until it's thick enough to knead with your hands. Knead for 10 minutes until smooth, then put into a greased bowl and cover with clingfilm or a damp tea towel to prove for 2 hours – ideally in an oven with just the light on.*

2 *Next, divide the dough into 8 equal balls and roll them out into 40cm lines, ideally slightly thicker in the middle. Shape them by bringing the two ends together, twisting twice and dropping over the middle.*

3 *Preheat your oven to 200°C. In the meantime, fill a pan 5cm deep with water (about a litre), add the baking soda and bring to a simmer. One by one, gently place the pretzels in the bath for 15 secs then put back on the baking tray. Once all done, slit them all at the thickest point with a knife and leave for 15 mins. Finally, top extravagantly with sea salt and bake for 15 mins until rich brown.*

4 *Serve warm with mustard or beer cheese and several pints of German Festbier, Helles or Hefeweizen.*

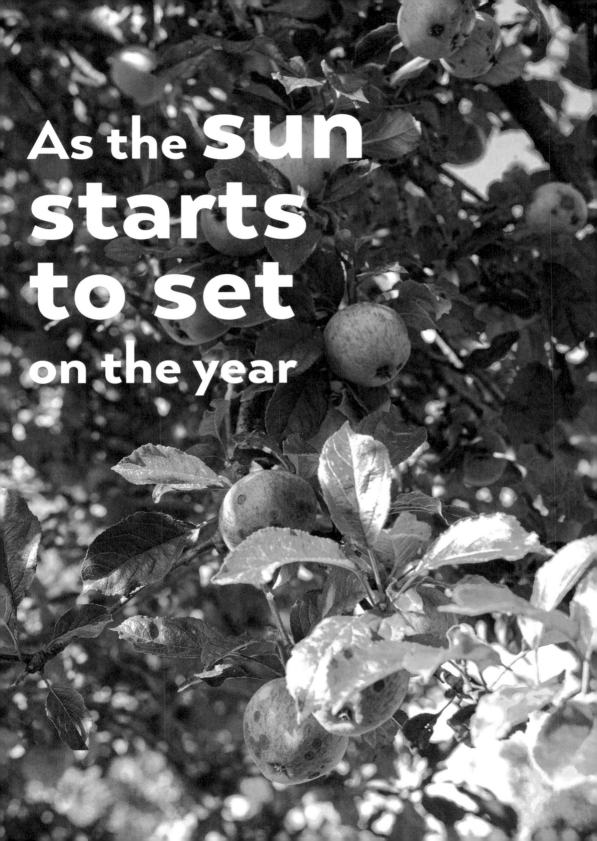

As the **sun starts to set** on the year

October

It isn't just leaves that cover the ground in October. We're at the tail end of harvest but there is still plenty of produce falling into our laps, most notably apples and pears. Cider has had a quieter revolution than beer, but the scene has changed immeasurably over the last decade. It would be easy to assume that it has ridden on the coattails of craft beer and small-batch gin, but cider has something both these industries struggle to create – a sense of place.

An artisan cider maker's connection to their base ingredient is so much closer than a brewer's, who likely sources the hops, malt and yeast from all over the world. Cider apples, meanwhile, often come from within the same farm or postcode as the producer, and are usually picked by the person who presses them, ferments them, bottles them and sells them. The cider revolution has also seen a huge rise in the number of producers using the wild yeasts and bacteria found on the skins of the apples, rather than adding cultivated strains. With only local microbes and local apples going in, a glass of cider from Hereford, Kent or Somerset will taste uniquely of its region.

Where making 'clean' beer means wrestling the forces of nature into submission, wild brewing and natural cider-making just require nudging it in the right direction. In wine they call it 'low intervention', but that's a little misleading, as I'll come to explain later.

October is also the most exciting time to be cooking and eating. All those fresh root vegetables add depth and sweetness to rich stews, traybakes and pies; and we're spoilt for choice when it comes to what we fill our crumbles and tarts with. The squash is perhaps the most dynamic and famous October vegetable. I'd love to say it's because it's delicious, but really it's because it's inexplicably become the symbol of the dead returning to the earth – and indeed of brainless zombie opinions about pumpkin beer.

What to drink

At this time of year I have cider on my mind – not just because of the harvest and the fact that the richer, tannic ones make wonderful Autumn sippers: especially if they have seen the inside of a whisky barrel.

When it comes to beer, the obvious answer would be pumpkin ale, but even the most avid fan can only do that for a few days of the month. However, Porters are very good at this time of year, being dark in nature but retaining berry and fig sweetness to suit the glut of delicious offerings of harvest time. It's also a great time to make the switch back to the cask pumps, having left behind the amber Lagers of Oktoberfest on the first Sunday of the month. Bitters and Milds make great session beers in a steamed-up pub, but don't feel you can't ramp it up a little.

October is traditionally a time for brewing strong beer and drinking the previous year's crop of big Stouts and Barley Wines. Most notably, Fuller's Vintage Ale comes out at this time of year and it makes a delicious accompaniment for ...

What to eat

... Cheese. As soon as the mercury drops enough that we all go inside for the evening, my first thought is that cheeseboard season is upon us. For some reason, around this time of year no meal feels complete without some cheese, crackers and chutney. It might be my stomach going into training for the holiday season, or it might just be that a cheeseboard and a Barley Wine is the absolute best way to watch the evenings draw in – tucked up warm and trying to tell yourself the bunch of grapes makes this a healthy lifestyle choice. More healthy would be the wonderful root vegetables that make for hearty roasts and warm salads.

Where to go

There are lots of real ale festivals around the UK in October – Falmouth, Nottingham, Twickenham and more hold their annual CAMRA celebrations. But the big beer event of the season is the Independent Manchester Beer Convention, more succinctly known as IndyMan. This incredible festival is held quite literally in the Victorian Baths of Manchester, and attracts some of the world's best breweries. It also makes sure to support up-and-coming breweries through its Thirsty Games competition, which means geeks will delight in seeing utterly unknown microbreweries pouring beer next to the likes of Jester King, Other Half and more.

Many of the UK's new cider producers have taprooms you can visit too, so head there to immerse yourself in the apple harvest and try some of that season's apples – the ciders themselves won't be ready for years, but there are always previous vintages.

A **cheeseboard and a Barley Wine** is the absolute best way to watch the **evenings draw in** – tucked up warm

The apple harvest

On the hunt around Herefordshire's orchards

As the giant Dabinett apple hit me square on the top of the skull I had two thoughts – one, that I should have been given a hard hat, and two, that Isaac Newton doesn't get enough credit for simply surviving his apple incident. The blow I took was enough to shake out everything I'd learned in the last three days harvesting and pressing apples with Little Pomona.

People often talk about cider and perry in the same breath as beer, but aside from being available by the pint, they have little in common. Really, cider is a lot more like wine. Craft beer now gets its seasonality almost exclusively through its wide variety of styles, created by the use of different yeasts, hops and malts that can be bought and stored all year round. Occasionally we augment these beers with seasonal fruits and spices, but even these usually come in puréed and preserved form to ensure consistency. Cider apples and pears, by contrast, are harvested once a year, pressed within days and aged in steel, plastic or wood for months on end. As a result, it has a vintage: good years and bad years; big harvests and small harvests. To someone from a beer background this unpredictability makes my head spin.

A few days shadowing Suzannah and James Forbes of Little Pomona taught me that things are even more complicated than that. I expected the apple and pear harvest to be an organised and bustling experience like the hop harvest, with lots of seasonal workers pulling 12-hour shifts and tractors flying at breakneck speed between the field and the press. In reality it's basically wandering, waiting, tasting and musing. Hops all tend to ripen at the same time, resulting in a mad three-week rush of hacking and drying, but apples varieties ripen whenever they damn well please. Discovery could catch you by surprise in August, while Dabinett might still be dithering in December. Even within orchards, within varieties, and within trees, the ripeness depends on the angle of the sun, rain and wind. Apples on one side of the tree could be dropping and rotting while those on the other side are still green and starchy.

That means autumn as a small cider and perry maker is spent driving between orchards to taste the fruit and inspect the trees, as well as quietly hunting down new orchards before your peers do. Such secrecy leads to myths and legends of hidden orchards and lonely trees that yield perfect pears year after year.

Cider apples and pears, by contrast, are **harvested once a year,** pressed within days and aged in steel, plastic or wood for **months on end**

If that sounds a little selfish, it isn't at all. It's all part of creating and sustaining the sense and taste of place that is so important to naturally fermented cider – that is to say full-juice cider fermented only with the wild yeasts found on the apples. Without a cultured yeast and only one ingredient to add, there isn't really a 'recipe' to consider. All the nuances you taste come from the variety chosen, the place it was grown and the time it was picked. Intervention in the fermentation process is minimal, and cider makers don't even decide the strength of the final liquid – the amount of sugar in the apples does that. All the maker can do is choose whether to age it in plastic, wood or steel, and perhaps keep an eye on the temperature. The art of cider making is mostly at the end of the process – in understanding how best to blend the different varieties and vessels. It's at this point that a producer can add or reduce complexity by playing with the different tannins, acidities and nuances to bring a blend to life.

All that happens years later, though. First, it has to be picked at the exact right moment. When choosing if an apple is ready, a picker is looking for two things – the 'actual' and the 'aromatic' sweetness. One is an estimate of how much sugar there is to ferment, and the other is a simple appraisal of how delicious the aroma and flavour is. The two are closely related, but knowing where an apple tree is on that cycle and when it will peak takes experience. We visited six or seven different orchards while I was staying, but only picked in three because the trees weren't ready.

Picking them takes no experience at all, though – simply a long stick with a hook, a bit of bravery (or a helmet), and no history of back pain. Pickers are constantly either stretching up or bending down, and carrying increasingly heavy crates around, and the pressing is only a little less arduous. Those heavy crates are tipped into mills that crush the fruit down into a paste to be squeezed by rollers or giant balloons. Over the course of a few days I tried a variety of apple juices – from the sherberty, sour Foxwhelp to the ultra-tannic but floral Chisel Jersey, as well as

I was never not full of **apples, tea and biscuits** during the day, and delicious **cider, pies and curries** in the evening

honeyed pear and an incredible press of quince that was like a citrusy pomegranate juice. It's almost a shame that all that lovely sweetness will dissipate during fermentation, but the complexity the liquid gains from time in fermenting is spellbinding. When tasting the juices you have to look for potential as much as anything, and the more delicious the fruit at the start, the more transcendent the final product might be.

That isn't always the case, though. When we stopped off at the famous Oliver's Cider to pick up some bottles, Tom Oliver proudly showed me the pears he was pressing that day. When he cut one open it was brown and bruised – well beyond what we'd want if eating them, but apparently perfect for perry making. Oliver would know – he is perhaps the best in the world at perry, and his Pet Nat Perry 2019 is my all-time favourite. It is so pale it's almost white gold in colour, with soft fine bubbles and a perfect structure of aromatic, juicy pear and drying tannin, complex but crushable. To see its humble, overripe beginnings was surprising.

Harvest time in Hereford is magical as a whole, but the best part is the evenings. Those who know and have experienced it come back year after year, creating a small wave of enthusiastic seasonal workers who exchange their labour in the orchards for tasty food and samples of upcoming vintages. It harks back to the mid-20th century when families would spend their annual holidays picking hops in Kent. Staying with Susanna and James meant I was never not full of apples, tea and biscuits during the day, and delicious cider, pies and curries in the evening. Each night was a new adventure into cider and perry, and how they interacted with food. On the final evening I discovered the match of a spiky, juicy blend of quince, apple and pear cider with artichoke-topped pizza, then we finished the night off with homemade brownies and a cider with sour cherries added – an absolute revelation.

However good it can be though, cider has some image problems it struggles to shake off. The first is the perception that it is not an artisan product. For too many years, larger cider producers have hammered the 'refreshment' and 'simplicity' line when cider should be a wonderfully complex drink. Capitalism made a necessity of quick fermented and lower-ABV produce that left wild, full-juice cider unprofitable. Now it's seen as a curiosity, and its higher ABV is a barrier many drinkers still refuse to cross. As James said to me, they have it all wrong – an 8% cider isn't a strong beer, it's a session wine.

The macro producers created another problem, too. The likes of Strongbow and Bulmers started splashing their marketing budgets during summer, when they hoped cider's natural crispness and acidity would appeal most to drinkers. That worked wonders for the bigger guys, but has really hurt smaller producers who rely on year-round sales and – again – make ciders that are too strong to be necked by the pint. It's a real shame that cider has become so seasonally restricted, but small producers are working hard to address the imbalance. Natural cider spends years maturing before being blended and bottled, then released either at their peak or when the maker thinks they will be received best.

The rich and tannic varieties are wonderfully warming and perfect with the richer foods, while those with heavy, boozy barrel character are perfect for the log fires and long nights that harvest time and Christmas bring. While few of these natural ciders and perries are below 7%, they make fantastic summery drinks when you might reach for a white wine. To me they are significantly more complex thanks to their myriad yeasts, soft Brett character and juicy body, without losing any of that crisp, clean and cold refreshing feeling. In particular, the table ciders that many producers make are great for this – they are designed to be poured out among friends and talked over, or paired with food without thinking. Because they're simpler blends, likely with no expensive barrel time, their price point is comparable with a good supermarket wine. That blows my mind.

The resurgence of great cider couldn't have come at a better time. The number of orchards in the UK has been dwindling for decades as they are replaced with more profitable crops, meaning many varieties have been lost for good. Given that the plants take a long time to yield good fruit – especially the perries – we need to keep the demand growing to encourage farmers to plant them for the future.

The fact that Susanna, James, Tom and countless other small cider makers are fighting all these battles and prejudices (on top of running artisan businesses) is why you'll never catch me referring to cider as low intervention.

Pumpkin beer

Halloween ales haunt us all

It started at Starbucks. Lots of bad things do. But specifically it was a consumer taste test, designed to help find some new seasonal flavours … because coffee just wasn't enough.

Starbucks director Peter Dukes was looking to inject some excitement into the corporation's latte range, and someone had the bright idea of recreating the pumpkin pie. It didn't test particularly well, coming in behind chocolate and caramel, but the flavour had one major advantage over all the others: there was nothing else to promote at that particular time of year. While a chocolate latte had to compete with a million other products at Christmas, Mother's Day and Easter, pumpkin has its own little October monopoly.

The product was perfected – which to Starbucks meant removing all the pumpkin and just using the cinnamon, nutmeg and clove – and put to market in the autumn of 2003. By 2015 they had sold over 200 million cups, and just about every other drinks industry in the world had noticed – including craft brewers.

I first became aware of pumpkin beer as a fresh-faced young beer geek in 2010, not by trying one but by logging onto Twitter. I'd never really come across the idea of putting fruit in beer, let alone spices, but even I couldn't comprehend the level of vitriol I was seeing. Quite why the release of a few hundred beers containing an innocuous and lightly flavoured squash varietal was causing a social nuclear meltdown was unclear. Were they taking over the market? Did the beers really taste that bad? Was there so much nutmeg in them that people were getting myristicin poisoning?

The answer to those questions (except for the last one, I guess) depends on your point of view. Pumpkin beer is just about the most divisive beer style there is. Some see them as an affront to the BJCP guidelines and the Reinheitsgebot – even to the common sense and dignity that beer drinkers are well known for (ahem). Others just think they're a lot of fun: they love the intoxicating spices that jump out of the glass and remind you of warm jumpers and crackling fires.

Increasingly, pumpkin beers need to transport the drinker, because they are being released earlier and earlier in the year. Like Easter Eggs appearing on supermarket shelves straight after Christmas, we seem to get a glut of pumpkin-inspired beers long before we get the actual harvest of pumpkins. I'd love to say that's because of the huge enthusiasm for the flavour, but it's more likely that breweries are just trying to get the jump on each other.

Most releases come in the form of a Porter, which is the perfect canvas for lots of heady, aromatic spice and the earthy sweetness of the pumpkin itself. But I've tried pumpkin IPAs, pumpkin Sours, pumpkin Hefeweizens, pumpkin Pilsners, and even a pumpkin Lambic. For me, the hit-to-miss ratio is roughly 50-50.

There are some breweries that are very good at it though, and Elusive Brewing in Wokingham is one of those. Pumpkin beers have never been as popular in the UK as they are in the States, where the style originated, maybe because we take Halloween a lot less seriously, or perhaps we're little more reserved about what we'll accept on a beer's ingredients list. Elusive owner Andy Parker, though, revels in the idea of taking controversial styles and running with them. He is a champion of the ultimately doomed 'Black IPA comeback' club, and regularly releases beers that most breweries would see the sales figures for and run a mile.

His pumpkin Porter, Carve'n Yams, is an homage to Elysian Brewing's Punkaccino. It takes direct influence from the original Starbucks drink, adding cinnamon, nutmeg, clove and roasted coffee, but also plenty of actual pumpkin, albeit from a tin. Parker doesn't know exactly how much flavour comes from the pumpkin purée (though it has a definite caramelised carrot note) so most of the beer's character is from the spices. He buys his pumpkin spice pre-mixed, but adds more cinnamon to really make it sing. All that spice – around 500g – and 12 cans of pumpkin purée go into the brew towards the end of the boil, while the coffee is added after fermentation, just before the beer is crash-cooled to drop out the hazy proteins. Parker then goes full Starbucks, adding a few litres of pumpkin spice syrup to the beer. Not only does that enhance the flavours, it provides simple sugars that the remaining yeast can eat to naturally carbonate the beer.

The result is a rich and complex beer that smells sweeter and more cinnamony than it really is. On the palate it's pretty dry, with lovely red fruit notes from the coffee and lots of biscuity malt. There is almost no hop character to speak off, but just enough bitterness from the roasted malt and Magnum hops to ensure the syrupy vibes are washed away. It's a beer that feels radically different across all its formats. In keg it's bright and heady with the cinnamon dancing off your tongue, while in cask it's more velvety and warming with the clove and silky sweetness really lingering. Both are really unusual and exciting flavours that suit the turn of autumn and cask format perfectly.

Pumpkin beer seems to have become a lightning rod for arguments around what is and what isn't 'beer'. But we have been adding fruit and spices to beer for millenia (gruit, anyone?), and giving those outside the insular world of craft beer a familiar foothold – even if it is one created by Starbucks – is a good thing. I'd appreciate it, however, if we could restrict pumpkin beer season to pumpkin season.

In keg it's **bright and heady** with the cinnamon dancing off your tongue, while in cask it's more **velvety and warming,** with the clove and silky sweetness really lingering

Cheese and beer

The world's most iconic duo

For me, happiness is a cheeseboard and a beer list. Add a long afternoon and a comfy chair and I won't stop until I've finished both – or fallen asleep.

As far as I am concerned, there is no better food and drink partnership. They both have such variety in flavour, strength and texture that there are endless combinations to play with, and yet the pairings are so natural that you don't have to think at all if you don't want to. You can treat it like a science experiment and marvel at how Bock, Kriek and Barley Wine can all go with soft goat's cheese, or just while away the time hacking away at a mature Cheddar while necking West Coast IPA. Both approaches have their rewards.

It shouldn't surprise you to hear, then, that cheese and beer have a lot in common. They're produced by similar friendly bacteria and (sometimes) yeasts, use local ingredients and recipes to create thousands of variations, and were originally farmhouse and monastic endeavours. I say 'originally' because both were mechanised by the Industrial Revolution, exponentially expanded and simplified to the point where they were unrecognisable, bland and hegemonic. This process of commercialisation happened to both industries at the same time, hitting rock bottom around 1970 with the wholesale takeover of factory-made Pilsner and Cheddar. To protect the margins, marketers and advertisers came in to sell the idea that these mass products were how beer and cheese had always tasted and – most outrageously – were supposed to taste. Thankfully, both industries are now repairing the damage, and the diversity we now see in beer has returned to the world of British cheese, too.

There are over 800 different known cheeses made in Britain, and presumably lots of experiments and one-offs happening too. Like beer, it has become a little tricky to keep up with them all, especially since attempts to categorise them are increasingly futile. My favourite example of this is the wonderful Stichelton, a creamy and salty blue cheese in a similar vein (excuse the pun) to the classic Stilton. When the owner of the dairy, Joe Schneider, first produced it he naturally wanted to call it Stilton – after all, he was within the area required by the European Protected Designation of Origin and used the same traditional methods. Unfortunately

There are over **800 different known cheeses** made in Britain, and presumably lots of **experiments and one-offs** happening too

though, Schneider was using raw milk, and despite that being more traditional – and arguably creamier and more delicious – that meant he did not meet the requirements. Instead, he named it Stichelton, the old English name for the town of Stilton. It is a very British way of throwing shade, and it makes me smile every time I think about it.

The more important point, however, is that it means we can't technically call Stichelton a Stilton. And it's examples like this that makes being a cheese writer (they do exist and they are excellent, eccentric humans) pretty complicated. So, for the purposes of my quick course in matching beer and cheese I will be making the kind of crass assumptions that would make said writers wave their cheese knives in fury. I promise, though, that the matches I mention will cause them to pick up their knives for their intended purpose, and get stuck in.

I am preserving some rules of engagement here, however. Sharing a cheeseboard is a fraught endeavour, and there are traditions to be observed. Chief among them is that you should never cut off the nose of a wedge of cheese. This is often the most delicious part because it comes from the centre of the wheel where maturation has happened slowest. Cutting it off is known as 'snebbing', and committing such a crime could result in your actual nose getting snebbed. You should take a slice an at angle to leave as much of the pointed end left as possible. I've also stuck purely to British cheeses, not because international cheeses can't be good, but because there is so much to explore from our own isles that opening it out further only increases the chance we'll lose our whey. I mean way.

The other rules are more like guidelines. I'd always suggest having a sweet and spiced chutney to hand, as well as either grapes or apples to refresh the palate and make it look like you are at least attempting a balanced diet. When it comes to crackers, personal preference is all that matters, but for the really mature stuff a sweeter cracker is usually better, while everything else benefits from something drier.

Finally, cheese tastes best from a slate board. Someone somewhere probably knows why, but just trust me on this.

Blues
Colston Bassett, Stichelton, Beenleigh Blue

Blue cheese is an acquired taste, but like most acquired tastes, once you have it you'll find it difficult to shake. The combination of cream and acidity from the white and funkiness from the mould – lapped by waves of salinity – is all-encompassing and heady. It does, however, require some seriously powerful beer to compete. Porters and Stouts are the classic match because they can add to the fruitiness while cutting through the cream and salinity with their roasted notes. But dark malts aren't the only option. A rich and amber Bitter – perhaps an ESB, even – works like a lovely chutney to soften the saltiness, and if you're feeling daring an English Barley Wine can do the same.

Creamy Mild
Tunworth, Sinodun Hill, Wigmore, St Jude

This group of cheeses includes those that display the characteristics of French bries and camemberts. The UK makes these cheeses just as well as the French, maybe even better, because we seem to have thrown a lot of the rules out of the window to get a little more variation. Sinodun Hill, for example, is shaped like a pyramid that had its top knocked off, and tastes like whipped cream and lemon meringue, with a slight berry note from the rind. Meanwhile Wigmore is mild, milky and ashy – perfect with a sweet chutney.

Whatever their individual character, these beers need a gentle touch. A sweet and honeyed German Helles is perfect, as is a Berliner Weisse if the acidity is restrained. These styles wash away the creaminess but perfectly enhance the lemon character. Adding fruits and spices into the mix can be wonderful too – consider a Belgian Witbier to concentrate the lemon posset note of Sinodun Hill, or a fresh Kriek or Framboise to estimate an American cheesecake vibe.

Creamy Mature (sometimes called ripe)
St Cera, Stinking Bishop, Baron Bigod

These are the cheeses you see people visibly recoil from. The kind that ooze like lava across the board when you release it from its wrapper. They're often farmyardy, orchardy and tangy – the sort of aromas and flavours that beer lovers expect from wild ferments and Lambics. That means that some of them are dynamite with those kinds of beers, particularly Geuze and funkier natural ciders, which have that apple vibe too.

You can have too much of a good thing, however, and actually I find many of these beers need the balance of something sweet. American Barley Wines loaded with liquorice and caramel can be fantastic with these funky fudges, but dark Lagers and Doppelbocks are a more sensible option. They have the malt background but also wash away the bold flavours with their snappy Lager finish, rather than helping them linger like a bigger beer would.

Hard Mild
Kirkham's Lancashire, Sparkenhoe Red Leicester, Gorwydd Caerphilly
The UK cheese industry has wonderful form in this category. These cheeses are somehow crumbly and creamy at the same time, combining soft acidity with flavours unique to each variety, which often has a strong link to the local area, climate and culture – or terroir as the French would say. That's why all of the cheeses I've highlighted as my favourites are labelled as 'British Territorials'.

They benefit from sweeter beers that fill in the gaps left by these very light and citrusy cheeses – Belgian Wits again fit the bill, but so do Milk Stouts if you really want to amplify that buttery crumble vibe. Red Leicester is a lot more earthy and pushes close to a mild Cheddar, which means a little bit of hop can be nice, but nothing too strong. A hoppy Golden Ale singing with the bramble fruits of British hops, or the elderflower notes of a lightly hopped Citra or Cascade beer can work really well. Caerphilly is the most acidic of these styles, and is a beautiful match with a young Geuze that still has a little sweetness left, or a fruited Berliner Weisse – raspberry would be the dream.

Hard Mature
Lincolnshire Poacher, Westcombe Cheddar, Old Winchester
This is my favourite category. When it comes to cheese, I love the mature stuff that finds cuts in your mouth that you didn't know about and has those amazing crunchy crystals in them that are a sign of a long-matured cheese. The other thing I love about them is the way they leave you reaching for a cleansing sip of beer.

I say cleansing, but really I mean equally mature and intoxicating. Because one of the key things to match when putting cheese with beer is intensity, so we need some huge beers. Barley Wines (again and always) go really well with these cheeses, especially the American kind that are really well hopped, but if you want to keep the ABV sensible and strongly hopped American Brown ale can bring out the natural nuttiness of these cheeses beautifully. The best style, however, has to be West Coast IPA. Their sticky resin is like honey, the citrus notes match the top notes of the cheese, and their bitterness really heightens that biting maturity on the finish. It's the kind of combination that leaves you reeling, sweating beneath the eyes and gasping for breath, wondering how anyone could enjoy such a thing. And then you do it again. And again.

Apple and Porter chutney

Great cheese deserves great condiments

For me, the chutney on a cheeseboard is just as important as the cheese. This is especially true when serving beer with it. A good chutney brings an element of sweetness so rarely found in dairy, while also working as a go-between to unite the beer and cheese.

This chutney is incredibly easy to make but can elevate just about anything you add it to thanks to how aromatic it is. Using a Porter adds a sweet chocolate and fig kind of note to the tart apples and vinegar, while the heavy use of Indian spices makes it sing from the moment you open the jar. It's brilliant with mature hard and milder soft cheese as well as simpler cured meats, but you could also use it as a dip for poppadoms, to jazz up a gravy, or just in a classic ham and Cheddar sandwich.

This is one of my favourite beer recipes, a fact only enhanced by the combination of the beer sent most commonly to India during colonial times with the key spices of that great nation's food.

INGREDIENTS

360g apples (i.e., about 3-4 apples), peeled, cored and cut into 1-cm pieces

125g raisins

1 onion, peeled and finely chopped

1 tbsp mustard seeds

1 tbsp ground ginger

1 tbsp good-quality curry powder

125ml white wine vinegar

160ml Porter

175g light muscovado sugar

METHOD

1 Get a large saucepan on a medium-low heat and add a small glug of oil. Tip in the apples, raisins, onion, and spices and cook gently until soft. Add the vinegar, beer and sugar, lower the heat and simmer for around 3 hrs, or until all is reduced and shiny. If it starts to dry out, put a lid on.

2 Decant into (probably) four sterilised jars, cool and store in a cold, dark place. Once open, store in the fridge and use within a month.

So we **cling together for warmth**

November

November is a month so visceral I can feel it as it approaches. It's the first month where you get that cold, crisp morning frost, and we've reached the time where we have to make our own heat and our own light. Our hearts and our senses are filled with the ashen tang of wood smoke, the powdery dust of a radiator turned on for the first time, the heady mix of firework gunpowder and burger vans.

If early autumn is about the sights, then late autumn is about the smells and the rush of nostalgia that arrives with them. I've come to associate several beers with this wonderful time of year, and all of them make connections to a time before I was old enough to drink. There's the toffee apple note of a Dubbel, the smoky bacon of Rauchbier, the liquorice of Barley Wine – all best enjoyed while cooking up something comforting that you're going to eat with a spoon, or watching a boxset you already know most of the words to.

You don't have to stay at home, of course. The pubs are beckoning but the Christmas crowds haven't arrived, meaning the cosy chairs and spots by the fire might be free. There's nothing more bracing than a freezing walk before the blast of a warm pub. Wherever you are, the long nights love to bring people together, two things that food and beer are extremely good at. Combined, they make me feel warm inside even as the outside temperature plummets.

Of course, it could just be the Barley Wine.

What to drink

November is when the ABVs might start to ramp up. Our beer jackets need to be a little thicker, and as our food gets heartier and heavier our beers need to do the same thing. When I dig out my old casserole dishes and switch the oven on for the long haul, the beers I like to drink get more rich and slow-brewed too. For me, it's time to start looking at beers given complex and exciting flavours from long periods spent in tank, bottle or spirit barrel. There's nothing like the vanilla and coconut hit of a Bourbon cask, or the boozy sherry of a well-aged Barley Wine. Goose Island's Bourbon County Stout comes out at the end of November and is still world class, but there are lots of independent beers just as good. Siren Craft Brew are perhaps the masters of spirit-barrel ageing in Britain, but BrewDog, Glen Affric, Tempest and Buxton all make stellar examples.

What to eat

Now is the winter of your content. There are still lots of root vegetables coming out of the ground, and we're also well into game season which means rich, dark and meaty stews with buttery potato or celeriac mash. With Guy Fawkes Night at the start of the month smoke is also on my mind: so roasted chestnuts, hot smoked salmon, brisket and pork butts are fitting too, especially with a Rauchbier. If there's lots of apples leftover then you can't beat a wintery crumble either – amazing with a Kriek or Framboise.

Where to go

The beer festivals start to wind down at this point in the year, perhaps to save our livers for Christmas. But if you live in the South-West then the Vessel Beer Festival is a fantastic event with some of the UK's absolute best in a beautiful location. Torrside Brewing also usually run their annual Smokefest in early November, so if Rauchbier excites you as much as it does me, it's well worth the trip.

There are of course lots of real ale tents at fireworks displays, and local breweries will rely on busy nights like that. Otherwise, you're best off heading to your local and ordering something a bit stronger than the usual.

There's nothing like the **vanilla and coconut hit** of a Bourbon cask, or the **boozy sherry** of a well-aged Barley Wine

Imperial Stout and Barley Wine

Warming up for winter

As one of the colder nations in Europe's brewing dynasty, the UK has always had a special line in warming winter beer. The Doppelbocks of Germany had the occasional eyebrow-raising ABV, and by the 19th century the Belgian monks were having a bit more fun during fasting, but drinkers from the British Isles needed warming pretty much all year round.

That's not to say we didn't have lighter beers for general consumption – as we've seen, beer was often drunk in preference to water – but when it came to feasting or proper drinking, we went all out.

As we explained earlier in the book, until the late 1800s all British beer was what we would now call 'mixed fermentation'; that is to say the yeast the brewer added wouldn't have been pure, instead containing different yeasts and bacteria that made the beer slowly turn sour and funky. Some would be served before those bugs really took hold, and were therefore sweeter, lower in alcohol and less wild. That beer was known as 'Mild' because of its simpler flavour, but in terms of ABV if would have been around 6% or even more. Not all beer was drunk mild, either. Some of it was left to age further, and how boozy and wild the beer became depended on the amount of fermentable sugar in the original wort. Whatever the strength or recipe, though, it was mostly referred to as 'Stale' or 'Old Ale' at the bar.

Despite its vagueness – when does Mild officially become Stale? – the system made sense to drinkers. Variation in beer was mostly regional, so parts of the country had particular styles that dominated and you simply drank what the house had, whether it was dark or light, bitter or soft. At the bar you'd might a limited range of beers from which you'd chose either a Mild, Stale or a blend of the two. That is, until the marketers, as they tend to do, came along and muddied the waters.

At the start of the autumn, once the new harvest has been processed and stored, traditionally brewers all over the country – professional and at larger households – would take advantage of the coming cool weather to brew some serious strong beer to lay down and store. For obvious reasons, this became known as October

As one of the **colder nations** in Europe's brewing dynasty, the UK has always had a special line in **warming winter beer**

beer, and would be enjoyed at religious feasts and coming of age parties from the following autumn. By the mid-1800s, imported wine and spirits like gin were eating into brewer's volumes and threatening the national drink, particularly among the rich. In response, beer salesmen started using fancier terms for their strongest, aged beers and at some point in the 1880s a few started using the term 'Barley Wine'. Bass was perhaps the first to do it, but there are more examples of the phrase in adverts among retailers than the brewery itself. It does impart a more grandiose idea of what might be in that bottle, but in truth the difference between a Stale or Old Ale and a Barley Wine back then was simply who you were selling it to.

For a few decades the terms were used almost interchangeably, but today the marketing has won out. Stale and Old Ale are almost unused terms, while Barley Wine is adored by beer geeks the world over. Despite choosing a specific term for it, what defines an English (or more accurately British) Barley Wine actually is still up for debate. It's loosely defined as a long-aged beer with an alcohol content of at least 7%, but the exact flavours vary. All will have a bit of colour, along with the associated caramel, bread and raisin notes, but darker ones will have date and fig character too. The only clear boundaries of the style seem to dictate that it shouldn't have any real roasted character (that would take it too close to another style we'll get into in a moment), and that it should probably come with a good dose of hops. In olden times that reduced the wilding of the beer during long storage, but today it's used simply to balance the malt and alcohol sweetness.

The American Barley Wine, which is now seen as a distinct and modern interpretation, takes that a step further by combining the nation's biting, citric hops with the sweet malts to create notes of liquorice and caramelised orange peel. Being a form of Old Ale, it is, of course, a perfect candidate for further ageing, but unless the brewer intentionally adds wild yeasts and bacteria, the dominant process is oxidation rather than souring. In beers this strong and dark, that means an aromatic sherry-like note that grows as the bitterness fades.

Those tasting notes show why this is the perfect autumn and winter style. Not only is that boozy sweetness warming, it brings to mind the classic flavours of the season: toffee apples, candied fruits and Christmas cake. It's also magnificent with mature cheese of all textures, beef and game stews, and roasted meats – all the kinds of foods we like to hunker down and warm up with. Obviously, I've never been to one, but I like to picture the taverns of old with pewter mugs, smoky fires and song. Being such a strong style, the hallucinations get stronger with every sip.

Sadly, however, that booziness has held back the delicious and unique style from wider sale, leaving it to be overshadowed by another strong beer that shares its blurred heritage but has a more glamorous story.

While lighter beer was being rebranded as Barley Wine, makers of darker beers had found a more exotic way to sell themselves. As we know, Imperial Stout has its origins in Porter, the roasty dark ale most famously brewed in London where it offered sustenance and escape to its overworked street porters. Originally Stout was just a prefix added to Porter to denote stronger and more expensive batches.

By the early 19th century the Russians had developed a taste for British beer, particularly the dark, sweet and hoppy Burton Ale, and huge quantities were being shipped across the Baltic Sea. But in 1822, as international relations cooled due to competing global ambitions, the Russians introduced import tariffs on a wide range of British products, including almost all beer. Interestingly, Porter escaped the change, perhaps because of the style's international reputation and strong

Today, drinkers expect their **Imperial Stouts** to be full bodied, sweet and loaded with **dark berries, caramel, coffee and chocolate**

association with London. Whatever the reason, the volumes of Porter going from the UK to Russia increased massively as it filled the void of Burton Ale.

There's a widely held belief that these Porters were then made extra strong (or extra Stout) so they didn't freeze on the way over, but that doesn't really hold water. If it was cold enough to freeze a strong alcoholic drink on the ship, it would have been cold enough to freeze the ocean surface and block the trade route. It's more likely that the Russians preferred the richer flavours of highest-gravity Stout, and entrepreneurial exporters pushed this more expensive brew harder. They knew their audience: there was a large, affluent ruling class in Russia who lapped it up, and bought into the idea that only London could produce such wonderful roasty beers.

In a bid to achieve similar sales at home, savvy British retailers started referencing those oligarchs in their marketing, attaching the word 'Imperial' to the Stout Porters that also went to St Petersburg. A beer allegedly loved in the Russian Imperial Court would have been alluring to the aspirational British middle classes. It seems, however, that the term spread quickly to denote the strongest example of any beer a brewery made – hence why you occasionally still see references to Imperial IPA by brewers with a greater awareness of brewing history.

Unfortunately, increasingly turbulent relations with Russia ended up blocking the export route even for Imperial Stout. Combined with the fact that Porter was falling out of favour with British drinkers and that the First World War would eventually limit the ABV of British beers, Imperial Stout became more a curiosity than a style by the mid-20th century.

That's until it enjoyed a renaissance as part of the craft beer revolution. In the 1970s and 1980s American breweries were mostly reproducing historic European styles like Hefeweizen, Pale Ale and Porter. That led to some daring breweries digging out historic recipe books to try more ambitious styles. The earliest record I can find of an Imperial Stout being brewed in America is 1982 by Bert Grant of Yakima Brewing, and since then it has become a hype style among modern breweries wanting to stretch their brewing legs. It requires a lot of technical knowhow to manage large or multiple mashes, long boils, fierce fermentations and the delicate balance of flavours, and part of the original craft mission was to bring such challenges and their rewards back to the brewing sector. But with America leading the charge, much greater rewards were required. Today, drinkers expect their Imperial Stouts to be full bodied, sweet and loaded with dark berries, caramel, coffee and chocolate – increasingly not just the flavours but the actual ingredients.

The brand extension of Imperial Stout started with Goose Island's Bourbon County Stout in 1995, a giant beer brewed to celebrate the 1,000th batch of beer at the Chicago craft brewery. Inspired by a conversation with the master distiller at Jim Beam, head brewer Greg Hall aged a huge Imperial Stout in Jim Beam whisky barrels to add vanilla, oak and coconut notes to the liquorice and dark chocolate of the base beer. Bourbon County Stout was a huge success with drinkers, who had never experienced anything like it, but it was less popular with beer purists. The first batches were entered into multiple beer competitions but judges struggled to put it in a framework for their analysis. Sometimes it was disqualified, but occasionally it was lumped in with the speciality beers where it had to duke it out with fruit beers and unusual Belgian styles.

Eventually, though, a new framework was built around it, allowing its spirit-derived flavours to be accepted, judged and eventually copied by brewers all over the world. Barrel-aged Imperial Stout became the first style that people would queue for hours to try – just ask any middle-aged beer geek about their experience of 3 Floyd's Dark Lord Day, for example. Even after the sale of Goose Island to the world's largest brewer, AB InBev, the mania around Bourbon County Stout is remarkable. In recent years the annual release has happened on the capitalist nightmare that is Black Friday, the last Friday of November. Drinking a bottle is certainly preferable to running around the crowded shops.

Although it's now made in batches that would dwarf the annual output of most independent breweries, the beer is still one of the best in the world. If you can stomach the strong bourbon character that billows from the glass, you will struggle to find a more complex beer. The aroma is exactly like walking into the barrel room at a distillery, all sweet oak and sharp alcohol, and it warms you with melted chocolate and a soft ethanol burn all the way down. You can almost see the smoke from the charred barrel, feel the stickiness of the wort, touch the dark void of liquid. It's one of those beers I wish I could try for the first time again, and in some

The aroma is exactly like walking into the **barrel room** at a distillery, all **sweet oak and sharp alcohol,** and it **warms you with melted chocolate** and a soft ethanol burn all the way down

ways I can. Goose Island opened the door to a new world of brewing experimentation and hybridisation. Doing so inspired many more spirit-barrel-aged beers, and you can find breweries using whisky, rum and even tequila barrels to infuse unique flavours into all sorts of styles, including Barley Wine.

The acceptance of these flavours also kicked open the door for all kinds of new ingredients – from the perfectly understandable coffee and cacao, to less easily justifiable adjuncts like banana, peanut and marshmallow. Because they are often extremely sweet, Alex Kidd (writer of famous beer blog Don't Drink Beer) satirically

labelled these adjunct-laden dark beers 'Pastry Stouts' and somehow the name stuck. Some are delicious, but the use of exotic ingredients removes the sense of seasonality that straight Imperial Stout has. Strangely, the beer credited as the first of this style –Cigar City's Hunahpuh – was brewed in Tampa, Florida, which is an unlikely place to make such a dark, thick and wintery style. Many of these beers often lose their sense of place too. While some retain it by using local coffee and chocolate beans or roasters, many others simply further the global pick'n'mix approach to brewing.

As you can imagine, such Pastry Stouts are also a nightmare to match with food. While Imperial Stouts are a dream with barbecue food, heavy stews, blue cheese, creamy desserts and all kinds of chocolate, Pastry Stouts demand to be the centre of attention. They are best paired with friends, so you can all marvel at just how intense the flavours are and discuss whether they are natural or not. Mind you, a really good straight-up Imperial Stout or Barley Wine is so heady and intoxicating that it makes demands, too. You need to find the right time to open beers like Marble Barley Wine and New Barns Plain Dark Beer, before shouting for quiet in the room and just breathing it all in.

Some beers help make the moment, some beers are the moment.

Oak, smoke and brewing

The relationship between wood and beer

Given that November starts with Guy Fawkes Night, it feels right to talk about one of beer's greatest friends – wood.

The sights, sounds and smells of 5 November stay with me all winter, only thawing with the spring. The aromas of burger vans, real ale, and gunpowder take me back to childhood while the crackle and stinging smoke of bonfires take me even further back – they feel almost carnal, ancient and vital.

This kind of atmosphere – probably minus the burgers – would have been found in breweries until relatively recently. In the thousands of years that preceded the use of copper and stainless steel, wood was the most important material in making beer. It built the brewery walls and fermenting vessels; it fuelled the fires that roasted the grain and boiled the wort; it was the spokes in the wheels that transported the raw materials; and formed the barrels that held the final beer.

Brewing wasn't the only industry that relied on wood, but while the world has long since moved away from this porous and flammable material, breweries retained it in two key areas. You see, wood's two greatest flaws are also its greatest strengths. When it came to food, it was far from a passive building block or heat source – it imbued everything it touched with flavour, whether by touch or through flames and smoke when it burned.

Most breweries are now cathedrals of steel: conical chrome fermenters reaching for the heavens and connected by a labyrinth of pipework. But increasingly, either in their own space or littered throughout smaller establishments, you'll find white oak barrels or foeders, and you'll see – and likely smell – smoked malts in the stores of all kinds of breweries. The influence of wood in brewing is still visible all over the world – in the smoked Lagers of Bamberg, the Lambics of Belgium, the cask fermented real ales of the UK, and barrel-aged Imperial Stouts of America. Wood can impart its own natural spirit into malt and beer itself, or you might also detect the ghosts of products that filled in barrels before, from bourbon and rum to Rioja and Chardonnay. When it comes to many beers, wood is the fifth ingredient.

Beer and the Barrel

Without wanting to get too hyperbolic, the barrel is one of man's most important inventions. Made by a good cooper, it could contain any solid or liquid and survive long journeys, rough treatment and repair. Most importantly, though, it could roll – and that made the wooden barrel vital to humanity for centuries. There was a time when pretty much everything that needed to move was put in one. It was not without its flaws, however, and modernity meant it was phased out by metal and plastic containers that were cheaper to make, harder to break and non-porous.

Ironically, the wooden barrel would have been consigned to history if it weren't for its more delicate nature. By expanding and contracting with changes in atmospheric temperature, pressure and humidity, barrels continually draw in and expel small amounts of any liquid they contain. Each time this happens, a little of the barrel's wood character is infused into the liquid and a little of the liquid's character into the wood.

People have been aware of flavours that different woods and ageing times could impart in a liquid for centuries, for better and worse. As many producers of spirits, wine, cider and beer switched to fermenting in copper and steel, others saw the benefits of sticking to wooden vessels. Whisky is the most obvious example: although it is made from distilling a hop-less beer, it has little character until it has spent time in barrel. So much of that comes from its years in barrel: not just flavours of peat, caramel, dark fruit, coconut and oak, but that golden colour, too. Wood's role in the final whisky is so important that producers put up with the 3% of liquid they lose each year – known as the angel's share – to the sponge-like quality of the wood. In fact, brewers often benefit from the distillers' loss.

The vast majority of the barrels found in the beer industry have been used to age something else first. As we discussed in the chapter about Imperial Stout and Barley Wine, the rich character absorbed from white oak barrels can add layers of complexity to a beer, including anything from toasted coconut and vanilla to muddy peat and tobacco. All kinds of spirits are used, often to complement the styles of beer inside them. Tequila barrels could work well with a smoked beer to make a mezcal vibe; rum is fantastic with sweeter strong beers like Scotch ales; and brandy is a natural partner for a deep, fruity and tannic cider.

It's not just spirit barrels that are used though. There is a saying in viniculture that it takes a lot of good beer to make good wine, in reference to the fact that most winemakers will drink beer during harvest. So while writers like to play the two worlds off against each other, they actually have a lot of mutual respect and plenty in common. One thing they quite literally share is their barrels.

Red and white wine barrels have been used in brewing for decades. Despite extensive research I am yet to find the first time it was done, but Belgium's Lambic breweries have been buying barrels from vineyards for most of the 20th century, and likely beyond. It's probably linked to a rise in the cost of wooden barrels as industries shifted to other materials and coopering declined. Brewers, who didn't necessarily need fresh oak vessels, would have happily settled for second-hand ones from producers that had no option but to pay full price.

The main reason Lambic breweries still use them is that much of the wood character will have been stripped during their time filled with wine. These unique brewers generally look for two things from their barrels: slow oxidation of the beer, and as little oak character as possible. Some of these beers will live in barrel for five years, so too much tannin will ruin the balance and finish of the final drink. That's not just true of Lambic, either. I can still taste an Imperial Stout I had in BrewDog's ageing room that had been in barrel for a decade – it was so woody I was worried I might get splinters in my tongue.

But for certain releases those breweries do look to extract some character from the barrel. Cantillon is particularly known for experimenting with blends of Lambic from different wine, and even spirit, barrels. Every September the brewery sends out a special blend that is released all over the world at the same time, on a day now known as Zwanze Day. Usually the beer will involve an unusual fruit addition – grapes, rhubarb and oolong tea have all featured – but in 2018 the beer was a blend of Lambics aged in Italian Amarone, Chianti and Sangiovese barrels. Cantillon owner Jean Van Roy didn't intend to release such a simple Zwanze beer, but was excited by the character these barrels had given his base Lambic. He blended them to combine the fruity notes of the Sangiovese and dry, vinous Lambic from the Chianti and produced what for my money was the best Zwanze beer so far. It's

strange to think that the barrels that produced these singular Lambics are now probably just another oak vessel in a sea of hundreds at the brewery, their wine character now entirely spent.

Lambic is still conversative when it comes to using its wood, but the same can't be said of many wildly experimental brewers from other scenes. Rather than seeing barrels as a vehicle for slow oxidation and tasty microbes, many modern brewers look to extract all they can from the barrels and their previous inhabitants. Perhaps the most exciting and experimental barrel program in the UK can be found in Berkshire at Siren Craft Brew.

Their barrel room is the only one I know that isn't on the ground floor, and the barrels can't be stacked for fear of the weight causing a collapse. That affords you a remarkable view right across their collection of well over 100 barrels, which includes everything from light, zippy, white wine-barrel-aged Pale Ales to rum-barrel-aged Imperial Stouts that are touching the teens in terms of ABV. The aroma is unbelievable, and subtly changes as you move around the room and get closer to different varieties. That autumnal aroma of wet oak dominates, but so does the vanillin – a chemical found in many woods but most famously in vanilla itself. It's water soluble, so is slowly extracted by the beer to add an aroma that is brilliant in Imperial Stouts and Barley Wines, and can also be used to add depth to Tripels, Quadrupels and even wild ales, especially when fruit is involved.

For Siren, though, the real joy of barrel-ageing is the blending. Just like in whisky, some barrels mature so beautifully that blending would be a crime, but most are unbalanced and need rounding out by combining them with others. Siren's first ever beer, the aptly named Maiden – as in maiden voyage – was made in this way. Every year the brewery makes a giant ruby-coloured Barley Wine and ferments it in steel, before splitting the batch across the best-smelling barrels they have at that time – rum, sherry, port, bourbon, whisky, tequila. The final beer is an equation made of all those parts, and the blending day is spent trying to find something greater than the sum of its parts.

I can just about remember a night at the Craft Beer Co in Clerkenwell, London, when they put several single-barrel versions on next to the Maiden. I spent a happy few hours trying to recreate the final blend, but I can't remember how close I got because the beers were all at least 11%.

Beer and Smoke

It should come as no surprise that smell and memory are closely linked in the brain. We've all experienced that jolt of a memory, prompted purely by the aroma of something we recognise. Perfume or aftershave can remind us of old friends and partners; freshly mown grass of long summers outside; and of course the unmistakable, apparently generic, smell of school dinners.

When we detect an aroma, that signal is sent direct from our nose to the part of our brain that deals with memory and emotion. Not only does that make smell more closely connected to those things than touch, sight or sound, but it makes it more immediate and transportive too.

The smell of wood smoke takes me straight back to childhood; to long evenings spent in front of the open fire at my parents' house, watching Blind Date as the flames crackled next to me. Bonfires have a similar effect, fading in memories of freezing nights spent camping in the Scouts, or firework displays at the local football ground. The memories last no longer than the sparks from the fires, but the feelings linger like smoke on clothes.

These smoky memories feel more ingrained than most. After all, it was our ability to make fire that set us apart from the animals. It let us survive longer and in unlikely places; it lit the dark to protect us and gave us a source of delicious food. The reminders of warmth, light and heat aren't just memories, they are instincts.

That makes smoke and food a visceral combination, and smoked malt in particular has to be lived to be believed. Like many of the brewing processes and

flavours we consider niche today, almost all beer used to have a smoky element. That's because it took centuries to work out a way to kiln our malt without the smoke from the heat source tainting it. Even once we did, many breweries kept the traditions and practices going, continuing to make beers saturated in the volatile compounds of wood.

Most smoked malt today is kilned over beechwood, a large deciduous tree native to temperate climates. On one level the aroma that beechwood adds to malt is easy to describe: it layers smoky, nutty and earthy notes on top of that husky, oat cracker flavour. But that doesn't really do it justice in a finished beer. By the time it's mashed in, combined with hops and yeast, lagered for weeks and served cold and frothy, it has gained complexity and simplicity in equal measure. You see, the most famous smoked beer in the world, Bamberg's classic Schlenkerla Rauchbier Märzen, smells of smoky bacon. It is pure Frazzles from the moment you open the bottle to the second it touches your lips. On the tongue it unfolds to show toffee, raisin and brown bread, but still the smoke is intoxicating, fogging your brain and sparking your synapses.

For some drinkers that's too much to get past, but for others it's a reason to get up in the morning. The production of smoked malt is almost exclusive to Bamberg, but there are plenty of breweries around the world who use it. Mostly it's a small portion of the malt bill in strong, dark beer like an Imperial Stout, and in moderation it can tease out notes of leather and tobacco, and accentuate the dry toasted malt notes. Some breweries, however, want to put that phenomenal smoky character front and centre, like the Bambergers do. One example is Torrside, a small brewery on the fringes of the Peak District. Founders Chris Clough, Peter Sidwell and Nick Rothko-Wright are obsessed with smoked malt, and despite the limited growth opportunities in making such divisive beers, dedicate huge amounts of time and tank space to beers with a heavy smoked character.

On my first ever visit I almost expected to smell the bacon and peat before I saw the brewery. In fact, it looks like every other brewery, though something does hang in the air. Not literal smoke, of course, but the scent of it. It's hard to shift.

Clough can't explain where his love of smoke comes from – other than 'spending a lot of time outside as a kid burning stuff' – but he found kindred spirits pretty quickly, in two fellow brewers and a few homebrewing awards that convinced them all to take it seriously. They started safe enough in 2014, making batches of Bitter for the local market, but after the first smoked Stout went down well with the public, it became the focus. Since then the brewery has made over thirty different smoked beers across a range of different styles, from Porters to Imperial Stouts, via Saison and even a few IPAs.

Clough seems to take pride in being contrarian and unexpected. The variation is so wide I feel bad for trying to claim that smoked beer straddles the time of year between autumn and winter. They would, of course, have been produced year round, albeit with a break at the warmest time of year. Many would have been designed for summer and taste just as good then. For example, Torrside have released their interpretation of an almost-extinct Polish beer style called Grodziskie

– a highly carbonated, light and zippy sour beer made with oak-smoked wheat. The style was hugely popular in Poland until after the Second World War, when the USSR nationalised beer production and closed breweries that weren't making the styles required. By 1993 there were no breweries making the beer, and Torrside is one of the few breweries making it today.

Torrside also likes to use peat-smoked malt, the earthy flavour so powerful that they have to crush it on a homebrew mill to avoid tainting their main mill forever. Interestingly, though, sometimes more smoked malt can end up being less in the final beer. Smoke itself needs a surface to play off, and other aromas and flavours to add depth to. Think about it in terms of a barbecue – the smoke from the wood chips doesn't smell as delicious as it does combined with the meat when you taste it. Smoke on its own loses its complexity. Generally, Torrside doesn't use more than around 85% smoked malt, adding complexity with other malts for the remainder of the bill.

Some of their smoked creations don't even use smoked malt at all. Instead they love to use old peated whisky casks, bringing together the two vital roles that wood still has in alcohol production. Despite the secondary nature of that smoky flavour, they still have to be cautious. Where most beers would sit in barrel for six months or more to gain enough spirit or wine character, Clough says a peated whisky cask can dominate a beer in just a few weeks.

The wonderful thing about using wood as a flavour in brewing is how it connects us to our brewing roots. Sometimes the next big thing is behind, not in front. There is an in-built attachment in us as humans to fire, to smoke, to char. Embracing it, particularly at this time of year, can leave us feeling more connected to our current surroundings and our past. It goes beyond that short journey from nose to memory centre: it goes to the heart of being human.

Imperial Stout brownies

As decadent as it gets

Brewing is a lot like baking. You can have the most amazing flavour idea ever conceived, but if you don't have the chemistry to back it up, it won't work. In brewing it's about water chemistry, yeast counts and IBUs, while with baking it's about protein levels, rising agents and moisture content. Whether these two professions are an art or a science is an age-old debate, but the truth is they're both.

Not so of the brownie. It is a recipe so wickedly simple that it will forgive even the most basic baking mistake, and that's how I stumbled across this recipe while coming up with some beer-themed pudding ideas. Not only does the addition of booze seem to make these brownies fudgier and harder to get wrong, but the use of an Imperial Stout really adds to the depth of flavour – whether that's bourbon barrel, coffee or marshmallow is down to how crazy the Stout is.

A lot of cooking-with-beer recipes are accused of being pointless because you can't taste the beer. Usually my response is 'can you taste the wine in a risotto?', but this is one recipe where you absolutely can taste it. There's also plenty of beer leftover for the chef, so keep it for when the brownies are cool enough to eat and enjoy as some overindulgence on a cold winter night.

A quick note on the toppings. I've used Biscoff because in my humble opinion they are the best biscuit in the world, and this recipe is amazing with a Coffee Stout. But you can totally leave this plain or add your favourite baked good.

INGREDIENTS

165ml/half a can Imperial Stout (the sillier the better)

180g salted butter

270g dark chocolate

225g sugar

110g flour

40g quality cocoa

3 eggs

4 Biscoff biscuits

METHOD

1 *Pour the beer into a medium saucepan and gently heat for 10 mins to knock out the carbonation, then remove from the hob and add the butter and chocolate. Stir until melted, then mix in the sugar, flour and cocoa.*

2 *Ensure the mixture is cool, then stir in the eggs and pour into a lined 20 x 20 cm pan. Break the Biscoffs in half and distribute over the top. Bake at 175°C for 20 mins, so it still just about wobbles when you shake the pan. Leave to cool so it can set before cutting.*

The world now lit by **our own lights**

December

More beer is drunk in the month of December than the rest of the year combined. That's not an official statistic, that's just how it is in my house. I'm sure we're not alone either, as people all over the world use the phrase 'it's Christmas' to justify that extra spoonful, that cheeky upgrade, or that one for the road.

The greatest gift of Christmas is the freedom it brings. Most of our lives are spent abiding by rules both real and imagined, but at Christmas we throw them all out. It means going to the pub at four on a Friday, eating chocolate at breakfast, staying up late to watch bad movies. In fact, we only really consider the careless bliss of December in January, when we're counting the cost of it on our wallets and waistlines.

But we deserve and need this time of feasting. Historically, Christmas was one of the few times of the year where almost everyone could have a holiday, and today it is a source of warmth in the bleak midwinter. I find it's a great time to do all the things you've been putting off – reading that huge book, homebrewing that mince pie Dubbel, defining craft beer over a Barley Wine by the fire.

We can apply that abandon and freedom not just to how much beer we drink but the ABVs of those beers, with our antics kept in check by how well-lined our stomachs are. Suddenly 5% goes from a beer you'd be wary of to a steady sessioner, and the 13% Baltic Porter you've been ageing starts begging to be drunk. In my house many of those beers will be Christmas ales, branded (for better or worse) with some horrendously kitsch portrayal of Santa. But for me that's the joy of it – Christmas isn't a time for overthinking things, it's a time for embracing people, clichés, and beers roughly the strength of port.

What to drink

If ever there is a time of year to drink whatever comes into your head, this is it. Whether it's a massive IPA, Scotch Ale or Imperial Stout – hell, if it's the turkey gravy straight from the jug – I don't think anyone should stop you. However, for me it isn't holiday season without consuming at least one too many Christmas beers. My favourite Belgian classics are De Dolle Stille Nacht, St Bernardus Christmas and n'Ice Chouffe, but there are hundreds made in the Lowlands. If you want to try some UK versions, there are lots of spiced and fruited beers released around this time of year – look out for the seasonals from Northern Monk, Wiper & True and Weird Beard. You can also look to the more traditional regional brewers for something a bit simpler, but no less malty or robust.

What to eat

We all know exactly what to eat at Christmas, but to throw some personal ideas in there – I'd slice and fry your Brussels sprouts with smoked bacon and sage rather than boil them; add a tablespoon of chutney to your gravy for sweetness; and make a turkey tikka masala with the Christmas dinner leftovers. I'd also refer back to the sections of this book on matching with cheese and chocolate, as both skills are highly relevant at this time of year.

Where to go

Christmas markets rarely stock great beer – usually it will be some mass produced German Lager, or worse, some mass produced British Lager pretending to be German. So when you're done shopping, swerve the fairy-lit tents and over-stewed mulled wine and find the nearest cosy pub for some real ale and a plate of pub chips. There's also the magnificent Pig's Ear festival at the Round Chapel in Hackney, London, on the first weekend. It truly is one of the best CAMRA festivals, perfectly blending ultra-modern brewing with historic styles and a great mix of generations and genders.

When you're done shopping, **swerve the fairy-lit tents** and over-stewed mulled wine and find the **nearest cosy pub** for some real ale and a plate of pub chips

Christmas beer

Embrace this celebration of kitsch

On the face of it – or rather the label of it – Christmas beer has all the hallmarks of a cash-in. Most British releases feature a rotund Father Christmas, perhaps a little ruddy from drink, while others pull at our tinselated heartstrings with sleepy, snowy scenes that feel increasingly ambitious as global temperatures soar.

Often the liquid inside has little to do with the season – maybe some roasted malt, or a higher ABV – while the more thoughtful load up the fermenter with all sorts of flavourful clichés. It feels like some breweries don't want to fully commit in case they are left with lots of cinnamon-infused strong ale in January, while others over commit in a bid to stand out. I'd much rather see the latter, because Christmas beer has as much historical significance and seasonal affinity as any in this book. Perhaps even more.

The time we now know as the end of December has long been a cause for celebration – and if we've learned one thing through this book it's that celebration means beer – but the reason isn't the birth of Jesus on the 25th. It was actually because of what still happens on 21 December: the winter solstice. There are lots of indications that the shortest day of the year was significant for ancient civilisations, many of which worshipped the sun. While we see the winter solstice as a bleak, short and cold day, they saw it as the return of the sun – an event that would have been honoured by feasts with the newly harvested crops and that season's fresh beer. As Christianity spread around the world it absorbed these older festivities, so you can find references to beer brewed specifically for Christmas as far back as the 10th century – specifically the reign of King Haakon the Good in Norway.

Vikings had long feasted and drunk heavily around November and December in celebration of the end of harvest. The cereals would have been collected and milled, the animals fattened for slaughter or ready to be hunted, and the first beers of the new crop ready. They called this time Jul (pronounced 'Yule'), a term you might just recognise.

A short exile in Britain inspired King Haakon to spend much of his time on the throne attempting to bring Christianity to Scandinavia, while maintaining some more local traditions, like drinking a lot. Inevitably he combined the two, because people are always more amenable with a beer in their hand. Whether Norwegians

The end of December has long been **a cause for celebration** – and if we've learned one thing through this book it's that **celebration means beer**

noticed (or cared) that Haakon had combined Jul with a celebration of Jesus's birth isn't clear, but around 920 AD he made it law that farmers should produce a special beer for the season to share with their workers and neighbours. In doing so, he might have inspired the world's first official Christmas beers. I say 'might' because it's safe to assume similar traditions were being born around the globe. In fact, beer is so entwined with Christmas that its main protagonist – by which I mean Santa Claus, obviously – is involved.

Santa is an evolution of St Nicholas, a Saint born in the third century. He's best known as the patron saint of children (and for giving the generous but anonymous gifts that led to the tradition of Christmas presents) but he is also named as the patron saint of brewers. Now, before we get too excited, it's worth mentioning that old Nick has been named patron saint of … well, just about everything in the 1,700 years since his death – including perfectly normal things like sailors, archers and merchants, but also 'unmarried people', 'repentant thieves' and apparently pawnbrokers. His link to beer is as dubious as it is to those latter categories. While he is often painted next to a barrel, the origin of that story is not a fondness for beer but the time he apparently found the remains of three murdered children in a butcher's barrel and managed to resurrect them. Merry Christmas, I guess.

Whether St Nicholas enjoyed – or even ever tried – beer is unknown, but it's safe to assume that on his feast day of 6 December there would have been plenty consumed. As we've discussed at length in this book, Champagne has only become *the* celebratory drink in the last few decades, and the cost of wine means it hasn't always been the natural drink for the table either. That's especially true of the nations that didn't tend to make their own due to climate, landscape or culture – places like Bavaria, Bohemia, the UK and Scandinavia. But one nation in particular took Christmas beer to heart: Belgium. Its strong monastic tradition will certainly have played its part. I was fascinated to discover that Chimay Blue, the brewery's stronger Dubbel-style ale, was first brewed in the 1950s as a Christmas beer, but two less likely sources played a larger role in its ubiquity.

Let's start with the Scottish influence. In decades between the Great Wars, Belgian drinkers were pretty enamoured with British ale. The empire meant the UK had a huge export market, focused on the quality and longevity of its beers. This meant it had a glowing reputation for its ales all over the world.

In Belgium all British beer was seen as premium, but the nation had a special liking for Scotch Ale. This is a pretty loose style, initially characterised by the fact that Scottish beers were often sweeter and richer thanks to higher finishing gravities and the use of brewers caramel. They were also cleaner in yeast profile because the famous Scottish climate meant they were ermented at something approaching

Lager temperatures. The result was a gorgeous amber, bready and nourishing beer that Belgian drinkers seem to have fallen head over heels for.

That meant a booming export trade for Scottish brewers such as McEwan's and W. Younger & Co (both of Edinburgh) through until the mid-1900s. An interesting thing happens around the turn of the century though. Examples of 'Christmas Beer' started being advertised in reference to Scotch Ales in Belgian cafés. This was remarkable for two reasons – the first is that the advertising was in English, and the second was that there is no record of 'Christmas' beers being brewed in Scotland at the time. It seems that Belgian importers had started relabeling the October-brewed imports – which would have been the strongest ales from the previous year – for Christmas, keeping the English translation to sell the lie a little better.

Accompanied with a little scarcity marketing, this helped drive seasonal sales and was part of a massive boom in British beer exports to Belgium. In just twenty years the amount of British beer drunk in Belgium rose six-fold, and in response Belgian brewers attempted to copy the popular styles. Some are still brewed today (most famously Gordons and La Chouffe's brilliantly named McChouffe) and there's a clear flavour link between the original Scotch 'Christmas' Ales and what came to be Belgian Bière de Noël (French) or Kerstbier (Flemish). Unlike most of the nation's beers, they focus more on bready and caramel malts than yeast esters, as well as being darker and sweeter.

Despite the **simplicity of the Scotch Ale** being its defining characteristic, the Belgians haven't been able to resist throwing **all sorts of herbs and spices** into their festive versions

Despite the simplicity of the Scotch Ale being its defining characteristic, the Belgians haven't been able to resist throwing all sorts of herbs and spices into their festive versions, whether it's curacao or coriander from their Witbier or more unusual ingredients like cinnamon, thyme and liquorice. Some of them are acquired tastes, but not all Christmas beers are quite so divisive. In fact, one of them went on to take over the British beer scene for a period back in the 1990s.

Brouwerij Artois had been brewing for centuries under different owners before releasing what became its most famous beer as a Christmas special in 1926. Originally it was a local special, brewed purely for its hometown of Leuven, but Stella – a golden Lager named after the Latin for star – was a surprising commercial success and export began year-round just a few years later. It became one of the UK's biggest brands by the end of the 20th century, largely off the back of the incredibly successful 'reassuringly expensive' marketing campaign that set its stall as a premium Lager. Today, of course, the beer's reputation is in tatters, but in the inter-war period it would have been a star to follow. While flavour-wise there is little to connect Stella with the rich malt and spice of modern Christmas ales, it would certainly have encouraged breweries to ensure they had a speciality release ready for the festive period.

Whatever the history, Belgium is now the first nation you think of first when it comes to Christmas beer, and the nation's interpretation has largely defined what Christmas beer has become. Most modern festive beers include spices, herbs, fruits and other adjuncts to give them a special seasonal edge. In fact, many of them are simply core beers rebrewed with ingredients that jump out the glass and remind us what time of year it is.

It's got to compete with the **cheese, chocolate and huge meals** we consume

The best Christmas beers evoke that kind of moment without going overboard on the spice mix, though. De Dolle's Stille Nachte (Silent Night) is a hazy, copper Quadrupel-like beer dripping with rum and raisin, toffee apple, banana and toasted brioche notes that bring to mind a booze-soaked Panettone. Belgian brewers are famously shy of revealing their recipes so the jury is still out on whether St Bernardus's Christmas Ale uses spices, but it has a subtle apricot and date vibe that sets it apart from the classic ABT 12 and makes it wonderful with dried fruits, nuts and, indeed, Christmas pudding.

One of the best-selling Christmas beers from the Lowlands is Gouden Carolus Christmas, a Quadrupel so dark it seems to suck in the light from around it. The aroma has its subtleties, but they are hard to find amidst the intoxicating aroma of liquorice, akin to being sealed up in a bag of allsorts. It's not for everyone, but like so many successful speciality beers, it has a powerful sense of nostalgia to it. For me, it is a floral glass bowl at my grandma's place, in which I'd find all sorts of retro sweets and chew through them, staring at the Paisley carpet as I was told I'd ruin my appetite for dinner.

Carrying on the good work of King Haakon, the Scandinavian countries have also embraced Christmas beer, or Juløl as they know it. Unusually, many of the macrobreweries of Denmark, Sweden and Norway brew seasonal beers, which are usually dark and fruity Lagers similar to German Bocks and perfect with the traditional Christmas dinner of pork ribs. The smaller brewers take a more irreverent approach – To Øl can always be relied upon for something unusual, such as a cranberry Sour or an Islay-barrel-aged Milk Stout. I particularly enjoy Mikkeller's Ginger Brett IPA, which is a surprisingly clever flavour match.

In the UK we haven't formed such a tradition around Christmas beer. Perhaps our Church of England sensibilities made it feel too gauche, or maybe we were served well enough by the glut of 'winter ales' released by most breweries come the

colder months. These beers were never a style as such – examples are too varied – but they were typically stronger and darker than the year-round offerings, with some being harvest and October beers from the year before. Some have been relabeled as Christmas beer in the last few decades, but there seems to be less of an appetite for the unusual additions seen in Belgium. Young craft breweries seem far more enthusiastic about the tradition, and every year hundreds have a go at bottling the spirit of Christmas: with varying degrees of success. Northern Monk's Festive Star is a tasty, spiced rendition of their coffee Porter, and Anspach & Hobday has released a few different beers based on Pfeffernuse, the classic German Christmas biscuit – the Saison is beautifully peppery and gingery and dances on your tongue, leaving it tingling, while the Stout is a little more reserved and easy sipping.

Many of these new British varieties are delicious, but they are mostly session strength, which slightly misses the point of the Christmas beer. It's got to compete with the cheese, chocolate and huge meals we consume, and shout over the noise of kids having the time of their lives and the TV on loud for the grandparents. We get one chance every year to indulge ourselves in these ridiculous spiced and fruited beers, and I want it to be an event as memorable as opening the presents or waking up to snow. For that, I can't see past the Belgian classics. Just perhaps not Stella.

Beers at Christmas

A guide to drinking on the big day

There is only one Christmas Day tradition I hate, and it's one all beer lovers have been subjected to – the well-meaning-distant-relative beer box.

This is how it happens. You probably haven't seen said relative for a few years. Maybe the last time was a wedding or a funeral, when catching up consisted of 10 awkward minutes grappling for something in common. Or maybe you haven't caught up at all, and your equally well-meaning parents simply mentioned you had 'got really into craft beer'. Either way, at a loss of what to send you, they decide to buy you some fancy beers. Of course, being a beer geek, you have a very clear notion of what a fancy beer is. It might be a 12% barrel-aged Imperial Stout with cacao nibs; it might be a Lambic conditioned over 100% Schaerbeek cherries; or the freshest New York-made NEIPA. But your aunt and uncle probably have a very different idea – and even if they did have an inkling, they'd struggle to find it on Groupon. And so it is that, without fail, I end up grimacing through a thank you as I unwrap a few bottles of short-dated Hobgoblin every Christmas.

Christmas morning

Thankfully, I am always well stocked with alternatives for Christmas Day. It starts with my take on a Bucks Fizz that uses one-third orange juice and two-thirds Deus Brut, a Belgian Tripel made by Bosteels (of Kwak fame). Deus isn't just any Tripel, though. It's bottle conditioned using the *methode traditionelle*, otherwise known as the Champagne method. The original beer – spicy, briochy and bittersweet – is refermented and conditioned for 12 months using Champagne yeast, in French caves no less. There it's slowly rotated until the yeast is in the neck of the bottle and can be 'disgorged' before being sold. The result is a sparkling, excitable beer that's even drier than traditional Tripels and gains that fresh apple-skin bite of Champagne. For me, it is a better combination with the sweet and already very acidic orange juice, and means that two or three glasses can disappear before I've even tucked into the smoked salmon.

For that very reason, the next move in my house is usually plenty of coffee, because I have to prepare for the unveiling of the Hobgoblin, and that smile takes energy to winch up. From that point onwards, though, there aren't any soft drinks in sight. I like to sip on pale German Lagers while the presents are being opened – low in alcohol, soft in carbonation and with lots of sweet honeyed notes that go with the nuts being passed around. They're also great refreshment in a hot kitchen, which is where I spend most of Christmas Day.

Christmas dinner

When we sit down for the main meal, I crack out the 750ml bottles of Saison Dupont. This is seen as a leftfield choice by many, but I can't think of a beer more suited to Christmas dinner. Like most beer histories, the story of Saison is hotly debated, but the popular story goes that it was brewed for Belgian and French seasonal workers – or *saisonnieres* – in the 17th and 18th centuries. Each farm would have its own beer, made using grains, spices and herbs from the fields and fermented wild by the yeasts in the air. Most of these beers would have been brewed in winter and laid down to mature until needed in the summer. Each farm's beer was unique and connected to the locality – the origin of the phrase 'farmhouse brewing' that we now sloppily apply to all mixed fermentation beers.

Saisons as we know them today, though, are very different, and came about as the result of one farm having a budding microbiologist on site. The farm at Brasserie Dupont was founded in 1759, but the brewery wasn't added until 1844 and didn't get its name until the 1920s, when Louis Dupont was bought the farm by his father. There he brewed farmhouse-style beers until Sylva Rosier – his nephew and trained brewer – joined and introduced a new, single strain of yeast that made the brewery famous. It ferments a full 10°C higher than most ale strains, and produces a rich bouquet of clove, banana and savoury spice notes that would have made Saison Dupont unique at the time.

Today, thousands of breweries use that yeast to similar effect, but Dupont's insistence on keeping its original strain alive – along with a host of other traditions – means the beer retains a character not found in any other Saison. It's that caramel note and spice that makes it perfect for Christmas dinner: sweet to match the root vegetables and cranberry sauce, spicy to cut through the meat and rich gravy, and brightly carbonated to wipe the palate clean before the next bite. For me, the flavour of Saison Dupont is as vital to Christmas dinner as the turkey.

When it comes to pudding, remaining in the Lowlands is a good idea. Belgian Quadrupels are essentially Christmas puddings in liquid form – all candied fruits, raisins, and orange peel with hints of liquorice and banana to remind you this has undergone some serious fermentation. If you prefer a bit more roastiness, a strong Porter would have been traditional with this British dessert. Both styles are also magnificent with mince pies and brandy butter, and pretty adaptable to all kinds of cheeses if that's how you prefer to get the heartburn going for the afternoon.

Nightcaps

From there it all becomes a bit of a bottle share at my house, as curious relatives ask to try whatever it is I'm drinking. My final tradition is a bottle of my favourite Bavarian Dunkelweizen, the beautiful Unsere Aventinus, otherwise known as Schneideweisse Tap 6. It's a rich and dark wheat beer, combining the classic banana and clove aromas with date and fig malt notes. It's my favourite festive beer and a revelation as it warms to room temperature by the fire, slowly releasing yet more nuances in the form of plum and raisin bread. Usually I get to enjoy it while those with less stamina fall asleep in their chairs, but the last few years I've ended up joining them as the full 8.2% ABV takes its toll.

The best nightcaps are the ones that send you off to sleep in a haze of intoxicating aroma, like having lavender under your pillow, safe in the knowledge that the only thing on the agenda for tomorrow is doing the same all over again.

A festive homebrew

Bottling the spirit of Christmas

There is a small but growing secret sect in the UK. They meet on quiet nights in the corners of pubs and craft beer bars, where they whisper and take notes as they drink tiny samples from unlabelled bottles. At home they hang out with friends in dusty garages, with strange smells and steam emanating from the door. They spend hours on niche internet websites before getting strangely shaped packages delivered.

I'm talking, of course, of the UK's new found love for homebrewing. The hobby is not as pervasive here as it is in countries where commercial beer is prohibitively expensive (like Norway and Sweden), or in countries where until recently the beer was so bland you had to make your own (good for you, USA), but it has seen a remarkable rise in the last decade. Where in the USA the homebrewing scene inspired a revolution in professional brewing, in the UK it seems that professional brewing has sparked a renaissance in homebrew.

Basically only known to themselves and the small club they probably are part of (plus some very understanding partners and friends), there are now tens of thousands of people brewing their own beers using all manner of equipment and processes. In my time travelling around the country I've seen people using everything from kitchen pots and old dairy tanks to hand-welded three-barrel kits and £10,000 super breweries on wheels. Each and every kit is able to produce beer as good as any brewery, and the variety is quite literally wild. The joy of homebrewing comes in how you can tailor both the process and the beer itself to your own philosophy. While most focus on making homages to the beers or styles they love most, some focus on producing the kinds of beers no one is making. That could mean using their own fruits or yeasts from the garden, local wild hops, unusual recipes lost in the archives, or just madcap ideas they came up with.

The **joy of homebrewing** comes in how you can tailor both the process and the beer itself **to your own philosophy**

Of course, all-grain homebrewing is time consuming. It takes a lot of research and preparation, and a brew will take most of the day (especially if you're having a few beers while doing it). That means many homebrewers can't stretch their legs without time off or an excellent excuse, and so Christmas is the peak time for homebrewing. Not only do thousands of beer geeks fall down the homebrewing rabbit hole thanks to gifts of starter kits, but those already down there take the opportunity to throw their recipe books aside, roll up their sleeves and make the mad, probably awful beer that's been in their heads all year.

My most successful festive experiment so far has been my mince pie Dubbel. I took a classic Trappist Dubbel recipe – lots of raisiny Belgian Special B malt and some biscuity German varieties, fermented with the Westmalle yeast – but added a cake's worth of raisins and dried currants to the boil in a bid to extract their sun-dried flavours. I then took the same amount of fruit again and made a tincture with Demerara rum, which I tossed into the fermenter when it was at its peak of activity. In my mind I was going to end up with a sweet mincemeat vibe, with a hint of roast lending an earthy bite and the Belgian esters of banana and clove adding to the festivities.

In reality I got the recipe slightly wrong. There was a little too much roast, a shade too much bitterness, and arguably a little too much booze. But like all the best Christmas beers, it was decadent and ridiculous, and the small flaws were the reasons that it aged so beautifully for the next year. I put most of the beer into 750ml bottles, meaning a new tradition of trying it every year has been born. The other tradition is using the raisin-infused rum left over from the tincture to make Old Fashioneds on Christmas Eve.

If you want to give this recipe a go – I've tweaked it to perfection – everything you need to know is over the page

Santa Needs Some R&R

A rum and raisin Belgian Dubbel

7% ABV   OG 1.069   FG 1.012

Malt Bill

50% Pilsner Malt
25% Munich Malt
12% Cara-munich Malt
10% Special B Malt
1% Carafe Special II
2% Dark Belgian candi sugar

Adjuncts

250g raisins, roughly chopped
250g dried currants, roughly chopped
300ml un-spiced Demerara rum

Hop bill

3g per litre Tettnanger Hops (60 mins)

Yeast

1x Wyeast 3787 – Belgian High Gravity (the Westmalle strain)

Water Chemistry

London water with Calcium raised to 100pbm

METHOD

1 *Treat the water then mash in at 65°C for an hour, before sparging at 75°C. Bring to the boil and add the Tettnanger hops. After 30 mins add the Belgian candi sugar and 125g each of the raisins and currants and boil for another 30 mins. Chill to 18°C and pitch the yeast, leave at that temperature to ferment.*

2 *On the brew day you should also mix 300ml of Demerara rum and the remaining dried fruit in a kilner jar and set aside. After around four days, when the fermentation is at its peak, strain off the excess rum and toss the fruit in. Allow the ferment to free rise for at least 10 more days.*

3 *Cold crash to 2°C and leave to lager for at least three days but ideally several weeks. Then prime to hit 2.8 vol and bottle. Leave for another month to condition in bottle, then serve at 10°C with a mince pie.*

Breaking the cycle

There's a common refrain among beer writers and lovers that if you don't like beer, you just haven't had the right one. The thinking is that, with such a wild variety of flavour, there must be one out there for everyone's tastes.

But I don't want people to just like one beer. The whole premise of craft was to bring variety back to the brewing world, and encourage drinkers to enjoy all kinds of styles. For that reason, I think we can take that famous saying a step further: if you don't like a beer, you haven't had it at the right time. A Belgian Wit or Fruited Sour might persuade someone in summer, but on a cold and wet day in a country pub a really great Porter or Pastry Stout might make more sense. A Flemish Red might disgust someone just looking for a refreshing pint, but try serving it in a stemmed glass with a beef stew and telling them to think of it like a red wine.

I hope, if this book does one thing, it shows that the context matters as much as the beer itself. At the start I said that seasonal drinking didn't really exist anymore, but the opportunities have always been there. To take advantage of them, we need to remake the connections that industrialisation, globalisation and commodification have broken down. If we can look beyond the marketing, beyond our normal habits, there is a wealth of joyful experiences to be had. That's not to shame anyone who goes to the fridge or bar just wanting a crisp, cold Pilsner. All I'm saying is that not going for the default, or just drinking what everyone else is, or what was good last time, could lead to a much more delicious, intoxicating and memorable experience. It could also have a much wider impact.

Loyalty is an incredible phenomenon in beer, and something that breweries and their marketing departments have fought hard for. There have been dominant brands and styles since the Porter breweries of the 1700s built the first brewing empires, and that reached its peak with the pervasiveness of mass-made Lager in the 1990s. When craft beer came along, a lot of people hoped it would bring variation to British brewing, and to some extent it has. This book would not have been possible to write even ten years ago: there just wouldn't have been enough tradition or innovation. But the 2,000 breweries that make up all that diversity account for less than 5% of the beer made in the UK – and even within that tiny bubble most of it is American-hopped and increasingly hazy. The result is that we find ourselves in 2021 risking the same homogeneity all over again. We think we live in revelatory times, but we're just following the same cycle. Just as Brown Beer was followed by Porter, Porter by Mild, Mild by Bitter and Bitter by Pale Lager, if IPA comes to dominate the mainstream it, too, will be replaced by the next fad.

While I'm as big a fan of Hazy IPA as anyone, it does feel like yet another step away from the idea of seasonality in what we brew and drink. Always being on the hunt for the best IPA is a game of diminishing returns, with the improvements in brewing these beers being much slower than our appetite for drinking them. Despite using ingredients from the other side of the globe, it's actually making our world a little smaller and leaving us less connected to it. Writing this book has changed my whole perspective on how to get the best from beer. Finding the seasonal stories to tell wasn't easy, so it is through no small effort that I have managed to piece together the makings of a seasonal approach to drinking.

The incredible stories I did find, though, make me think there is a chance to stop history repeating itself. There is enough diversity and variety for us to break the longer-term cycle and move towards a more seasonal one. Globalisation – the very process that has resulted in us glugging Pilsner or IPA throughout the year – can have a very different effect if we embrace its ability to shrink time and space. In the UK we now fill barrels with Lambic-style beer in January, brew with ultra-fresh American hops in April, celebrate Oktoberfest in September, and import Belgian Ales in December. This means we can drink Bohemian Pilsner in taprooms in Lewes, down Maibocks in May like the Germans of the 1800s, and sip Baltic Porter on cold winter days. All of these phenomena help ground us in the moment and connect us to those that happened thousands of miles away and hundreds of years ago. We can be inspired by, rather than reliant on, the seasons.

That would be a wonderful paradigm shift, because craft beer has always looked to the future, endlessly wondering what's next without actually considering where it all came from. Think of the incredible journeys we'd all be taking if we understood the arduous, time-limited journey of green hopped beer, or understood the history of drinking Barley Wine in October, or enjoying a Porter with our roast beef. Following on from that, think how much more flexibility brewers could have if they knew that unusual styles would sell well if brewed at the right time of year. It would be wonderful to see more authentic Oktoberfests, green hop festivals all over the UK, hundreds of new apple and pear orchards being planted, a festival of harvest beers like Barley Wine, the rise of wild and farmhouse-style brewing in all corners of the country, and a boom in farming as demand for British ingredients soars.

This country is the home of great malt, but while the rest of the world knows about that we hardly mention it. We're equally dismissive of our incredible British hops. They can't give us the massive tropical notes of New World hop varieties, but why would we want them to? English hops aren't any worse than American, European or Antipodean varieties. It was only a few decades ago that American hops were discarded by brewers for their abrasive character and rough bitterness. By comparison, British hops are smooth, spicy and the only natural fit for the brewing styles we have here; styles so many old drinkers forget and new drinkers never discover because their connection and understanding of local ingredients is broken.

I don't want this book to be a one-off puff piece for the marvel of nature and beer production. While I have been really gentle with the political, social and ecological side, I hope this can be the start of a step change in the way that beer is viewed and consumed both in the UK and throughout the world. Following nature rather than resisting it is better for the environment, better for our society and better for us as drinkers. Chefs have done an excellent job of encouraging people to think more seasonally about the food they eat, and brewers could learn a lot from it. Concepts such as food miles, local cuisine, freshness, sustainability and supporting local farmers are all things that apply neatly to brewing, too. I'd hate to see imported beer disappear from the UK – they have their own seasonality to them, too – but I would love the variety of beers available in the UK to reflect our climate, culture and history more than it does right now.

That starts with me and you. Every brewer I spoke to for this book lamented the fact they couldn't brew broader styles, or the beers they loved to drink themselves in bigger volumes. The commercial reality of demand is hampering creativity, and encouraging homogeneity, which excludes people who don't love those dominant styles and reinforces the idea that other styles aren't as good. The truth is I am not sure there is space for 2,000 IPA-based craft breweries in the UK, and I am certain that macro breweries are already muscling in and starting to shrink that space. Without something changing, our obsession with certain styles and processes could come back to haunt us.

As consumers, the best way we can help is to drink seasonally and support breweries that embrace the challenges and the joys of thinking in this way. Not only does our long-term enjoyment of beer depend on it, I believe the future of independent brewing depends on it, too.

And so ends a year in beer.
But the adventure doesn't stop here.

I also filmed many of the adventures I had while writing this book, and the videos are available on the **Craft Beer Channel** or if you scan ⟵·········· this QR code.

CAMRA Books

Modern British Beer
Matthew Curtis

This book is about why modern British beer is important. Over the course of the past two decades the brewers of Great Britain and Northern Ireland have carved out a unique and world-leading beer culture. Matthew Curtis guides you on a journey of discovery across the British Isles, discovering a beer culture that is world-beating but also intrinsically local at heart. Through the stories of 86 different beers, he gives a personal insight into birth of Modern British Beer; from how it tastes, to where its ingredients are from, to the people behind the scenes working hard to make it.

RRP £15.99   ISBN 978-1-85249-370-7

Modern British Cider
Gabe Cook

Cider is one of the world's oldest drinks, with a heritage dating back at least 2,000 years. It formed an integral part of the landscape, economy and culture of many rural parts of the UK for centuries before being commoditised by industrial-scale production. Cider now faces a new change in the drinking landscape of Britain – the rise of craft drinks, which brings with it modern, discerning drinkers with different needs, habits and spending opportunities. Acclaimed cider expert Gabe Cook celebrates the heritage, diversity and innovation within the wonderful world of British cider today.

RRP £15.99   ISBN 978-1-85249-371-4

World Beer Guide
Roger Protz

The world of beer is on fire. Traditional brewing countries are witnessing a spectacular growth in the number of beer makers while drinkers in such unlikely nations as France and Italy are moving from the grape to the grain. Drawing on decades of experience, Roger Protz takes readers on a journey of discovery around the world's favourite alcoholic drink – uncovering the interlinked stories behind the best breweries and beers across every continent in the world.

RRP £30   ISBN 978-1-85249-373-8

Order these and other CAMRA Books from **shop.camra.org.uk**